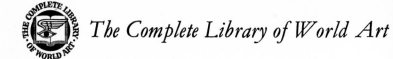
The Complete Library of World Art

ALL THE PAINTINGS

OF **PAOLO UCCELLO**

Text by ENZO CARLI

Translated from the Italian by
MARION FITZALLAN

HAWTHORN BOOKS, INC.

Publishers · New York

Manufactured in Great Britain by Jarrold & Sons Ltd, Norwich

CONTENTS

NOTE

In the spring and summer of 1954 (April 22 to July 31) an exhibition of Four Early Renaissance Masters was held in the Palazzo Strozzi in Florence, under the chairmanship of Mario Salmi. The Exhibition included an important group of works by Uccello and his followers. I did not, however, modify what I had written before because the problems raised by the Exhibition are of too specialized a nature to be dealt with in this book. Nevertheless, I draw the reader's attention to the careful assessment of Uccello edited by Emma Micheletti for the Catalogue of the Exhibition (Florence, 1954), and also to restorations of the Uffizi panel of *The Battle of San Romano*, and *The Profanation of the Host*, both of which were prepared for this occasion.

E.C.

PAOLO UCCELLO

Life and Work

PAOLO di DONO, known as Paolo Uccello, is one
of the fifteenth-century Florentine artists who have
most excited the interest and curiosity of modern
critics.

Uccello is perhaps the most problematic personality in
Italian art. He has never been completely forgotten; he has
not been "rediscovered" by modern studies, nor reassessed
in the light of recent aesthetic theories or artistic fashions.
He is not categorized as a genius, nor is he admired despite
limitations. To clarify this, we might take as an example an
artist from the same century, Benozzo Gozzoli, an artist of
infinitely less stature than Uccello. Yet Gozzoli lies peacefully in honorable mediocrity and does not seem to have
been as severely censured as Uccello. Authoritative critics
have said that Uccello was in the wrong vocation—perhaps
the most unkind thing to say about an artist (nothing of the
kind has been said about Gozzoli). Such severe criticism,
therefore, must imply other qualities, intellectual or moral,
but certainly extraneous to art, that are recognized in
Uccello. Indeed, it has been said of Uccello that he was "a
man with a scientific bent who turned to art." And by no
less an authority than the famous Vasari biographies, in a
revised edition published during a period of active and
intelligent criticism. Vasari supports his judgment by

quoting Donatello's words to his friend Uccello—that is, by quoting men in the same trade talking "shop" to one another. Uccello was showing Donatello "*mazzocchi* [male head-dress] that came to a point, and squares drawn from different angles of perspective" and other such exercises in perspective. Donatello said, "Ah, Paolo, with this perspective of yours, you are losing the substance for the shadow. This is for men who work at the inlaying of wood—these circles, spirals, squares and all!"

This, then, is the central problem in the interpretation of Uccello's art and personality. All other problems brought up by later critics are a result of this central question (and often unjustified additions such as the superfluous considerations about whether Uccello was a Gothic or Renaissance artist).

Obsessed as he was by perspective, was Uccello an artist or a scientist? Were his leanings toward science greater than toward art? Critics find his artistic personality contradictory and disconcerting. A dualism is thus acknowledged: an internal conflict between two different and incompatible forms of mental activity, one intuitive and creative, the other rational and inquiring. But many of the critics who have considered that Uccello's artistic experience was limited (in comparison with his contemporaries such as Masaccio, Brunelleschi and Donatello) have concentrated chiefly on his failure to develop rational principles of perspective, on his sporadic application of any principle, or on the illogical connection in his work between the representation of a single object and a vision of the whole. They have thus considered him an inferior artist because he was not sufficiently scientific.

But art can never be a strictly rational process, and although it reveals truth, it does not do so logically. Uccello, however, has been a victim of a misunderstanding of this function and method of artistic "reasoning." The pseudo-critical term, "naturalism," has been overworked in Uccello's case; he had an extraordinary knowledge of perspective—which is a science (or a discipline)—and a graphic practice based on certain optic, geometric and mathematical principles and laws. But this does not mean that he should apply perspective only with naturalistic ends, with scientific means and with a scientific mind. If he had been so limited he would not have been an artist, but a theorist and mathematician. This is true not only of Uccello but also of Brunelleschi, Donatello and even of Piero della Francesca (who in his old age wrote a treatise on perspective, *De Prospectiva pingendi*). Della Francesca, who had perhaps the finest mind of his century, succeeded in combining speculative and intuitive capacities to form a wonderfully unified image-concept of the universe. But he did not in any way subordinate his artistry, or his "fantasy" in searching for an individual form, to the rules of abstract, naturalistic or "scientific" reasoning. As Schlosser points out, perspective as such—a technical study —does not play an important part in Della Francesca's work as a whole.

The initial error was to consider perspective (which stimulated the creative faculties of fifteenth-century Florentine artists) as a complex set of rules with absolute values; an attempt, we might say, to rationalize knowledge of reality in visual form. Consequently, and referring in particular to Uccello, this standard limits the content and value of his art almost exclusively to facts of nature, and overlooks many other expressive elements. It is wrong to compare Uccello's experiments with perspective with the experiments of other artists of his time.

Some fifteenth-century Florentine painters, sculptors and architects worked with mathematicians and, for specific reasons, even became mathematicians themselves, and used certain principles and rules of perspective. But they were true artists and were not ultimately concerned with the validity or immutability of such rules; they did not repudiate them but merely extracted suggestions which they could interweave with another and very different kind of reality: their own aesthetic creation. Indeed, considering the considerable but extremely varied achievements of artists like Masaccio, Brunelleschi and Piero della Francesca, one is tempted to conclude that there are more perspectives in an artist's imagination than mathematics ever dreamed of!

But what did perspective mean for Uccello? It was certainly not an arid discipline that might conceivably have led to an artistic paradise; not a kind of rational conquest by a man who was already a scientist. It was something "fine" which inspired and consoled him even in old age and disillusionment. It suggested to his imagination a world of beckoning forms in which reality and imagination were miraculously transformed by a logic that was consonant with the deepest impulses of his being. It gave him pleasure and freed him from everyday reality.

Uccello's perspective has an exclusively lyrical character, and is remote from representative illusion. This is revealed by what is generally accepted to be his major achievement in perspective: the fresco depicting *The Flood* in the Chiostro Verde of the Convent of Santa Maria Novella in Florence (plate 44). But if, indeed, perspective was meant to give more reality to the event by determining spatial unity, Uccello would not—with "medieval" ingenuity—have combined two distinctly separate incidents in a single visual scene which is contained within the same well-defined space. Clearly Uccello's training contradicted this; he knew that because of the requirements of perspective it is impossible to represent any single scheme with numerous separate vanishing points and with numerous converging lines of perspective. Yet he did just this in *The Nativity* in the ex-Hospital of San Martino alla Scala (plate 61). Here two different, diverging representations of space branch off behind the shoulders of the Virgin kneeling in the foreground. In both cases, perspective enabled Uccello to obtain a new spatial dimension whose linear formation is brilliantly assertive, clear and regular. This also applies to the positions of individual objects and figures. All show a tendency, if not to the abstract purity of Euclid's solids, at least toward geometrical expression and toward eloquence in their clearly defined profiles. Uccello was an artist in linear perspective, and this was natural since he grew up in Ghiberti's workshop, where he was first employed as an errand-boy at the age of ten, in 1407.

There is unfortunately no record of his youthful activities. The first mention is his return to Florence from Venice about 1431. But it is possible to reconstruct the formation of his early personality through the artistic events with which he was in contact and which must have interested him during the "blank" period in Florence—from his birth in 1397 until 1425, and later in Venice until 1430. This reconstruction has been masterfully done by John Pope-Hennessy and Mario Salmi. In Ghiberti's goldsmith shop—the most famous, sophisticated artistic meeting-place for the first twenty years of the century—were a few outstanding champions of Florentine Late Gothic art. It is better to describe this style as Gothic, for, rather than becoming international and therefore diffuse, it remained cloistered—exemplified by the linear lyricism of Lorenzo Monaco—or it renewed primitive anchorite forms with painters like Gherardo Starnina. The scenes of contained and colorless processions now saw brighter participants and more cosmopolitan style: a world of pageantry, of luxuriously dressed fair cavaliers; lively, richly harnessed horses, their backs gleaming and their necks arched proudly; slender greyhounds, trained to hunt by night; soldiers in shining armor; exotic animals and birds. All the pageantry that informed the *Adoration of the Magi* painted in 1423 by the Venetian artist, Gentile da Fabriano, for the Church of Santa Trinità, which enchanted all Florence. This world fascinated Paolo di Dono (he had not yet acquired his last name, Uccello, or "bird"). Soon after Gentile da Fabriano had completed the *Quaratesi Polyptych* in the Church of San Niccolò, Uccello set out to discover this fabulous world of chivalry for himself. He found it in the Book of Hours and in an Herbarium which, in a city where Masaccio's genius had yet to emerge fully, must have seemed the latest advance in painting.

Having made a will, Uccello left for Venice on August 5, 1425. This first stay in Venice had some influence in the formation of his taste. It appears that he received a commission for a mosaic for St Mark's. He must have enjoyed the neat, exact technique required by this work, with its vividly colored pieces and precise contours. We do not know much about his success in this genre. Salmi, however, points out that Gentile Bellini's *Procession of the Relic of the Cross in St Mark's Square* has definite reminders of Uccello's *St Peter* which was executed in mosaic on the façade of St Mark's. It is a huge, robust, well-set figure which reveals perhaps Uccello's homage to the sculptor, Ghiberti.

Uccello must have been even more impressed by the (now lost) frescoes by Gentile da Fabriano (and Pisanello) in the Great Council Chamber of the near-by Ducal Palace. Here, too, he would have admired the "interweaving of galleys and furious fighters" in Gentile's legendary *Battle of Punta Salvore* with its terrifying vision of a hurricane *"arbores ceteraque id genus radicibus evertentem."* These impressions were surely decisive. They must have matured slowly in the artist's consciousness; he may have remembered them when executing the armed crowds in the three panels of *The Battle of San Romano* (plates 68–69, 80–81 and 92–93), and in the stormy background of *The Flood* (plate 44). Matured slowly, that is, because after he returned to Florence there is no evidence in his first works there to suggest that he had ever left the city.

These are the four stories from Genesis (plate 1), frescoed in *terra verde* (a natural green earth) in the Cloister of the Convent of Santa Maria Novella. The frescoes are: *The Creation of the Animals* and *The Creation of Adam* placed in a small lunette; *The Creation of Eve* and *The Fall* placed in an oblong space beneath, the two groups separated by a narrow black and white ledge.

During Uccello's absence much had happened in Florence. By this time (1430–31) Masaccio was dead, Brunelleschi had carried out some of his most revolutionary ideas in architecture, and a new race of plebeian-looking Prophets was settling down in the niches of Giotto's Campanile. But Uccello was concerned only with his first master, Ghiberti. He took as an example for the figure of Adam (plate 3) an analogous panel in Ghiberti's *Door of Paradise*. He made use of the drapery of *St Matthew* in Orsanmichele for his Eternal Father; and the balanced figures of Adam and Eve in *The Fall* (plate 8) reflect a Ghibertian rhythm. In the two first scenes of the stories from Genesis he was still interpreting the relationship between figures and landscape with a "Gothic" and Ghiberti-like feeling. The landscape (especially in *The Creation of Adam*), with its curving outlines, echoes and diminishes the outlines of the figures which—as far as one can judge now—were executed with strong plasticity from which irradiating lines gradually become softer and more fragmentary. Barren rocks with their edges steeped in cold light—as in night backgrounds by Lorenzo Monaco—are interspersed with bare, straight coniferous trunks similar to those in the panels of the *Door of Paradise*. In the two scenes below, the rich foliage, dotted with spherical fruit, is —as Salmi has noted—reminiscent of the minute attention to detail in Franco-Flemish tapestry and in International Gothic frescoes "regenerated through regular forms in a perfection that surpasses reality." The female head of the serpent projects from the leaves like a golden-pink fruit; the precision of her profile reminds one of a medallion by Pisanello; and there is perfect rhythmic conformity between her luminous convex forehead and arching shadowed brows, between the pointed chin, the chiseled ear gleaming like a jewel in her soft hair (plate 9). This, Uccello's first masterpiece, is derived from the same geometric spirit that was to appear a few years later on a monumental scale in the equestrian portrait of *Sir John Hawkwood* (plate 10), executed in 1436 for the Church of Santa Maria del Fiore, the Duomo.

A beautiful squared preliminary drawing in the Uffizi (plate 116) gives a clearer indication of the artist's original intentions. It has no naturalistic aims but concentrates on developing a play of full, curved outlines. In the drawing— and not only because there is no chiaroscuro here—these outlines are more closely knit and more precise than in the final painted version. The fresco was damaged and was retouched—if not totally repainted (as Longhi supposes)— by Uccello himself about 1455; the candelabra on the frame have certainly been repainted.

The Florentines' first intention had been to honor their

leader, Sir John Hawkwood, with a marble statue. Although the idea of a marble monument was soon afterwards abandoned in favor of a frescoed tomb (executed in 1395 by Agnolo Gaddi and Giuliano d'Arrigo), Uccello certainly had sculptural examples in mind when he executed his fresco: above all, the Alexandrian gilded bronze horses that had come from Constantinople and had been placed as war trophies on the façade of St Mark's in Venice.

Yet even while reproducing an ideal bronze monument and clearly searching for plastic and monumental sculptural effects, Uccello created an exclusively pictorial, linear form. So (leaving to cavalry colonels the secular discussion on the inexactitude of the horse's walk—later interpreted as an "ambling pace"), the contradiction in perspective between the equestrian group and the base seems to be motivated by Uccello's desire for balance between the majestic, geometrical development of horse and rider, and the architectural projection and ornamentation on the base. The eye of the observer, roughly level with the horse's cannons, sees this balance in all its conclusive formal unity, extending to the horse's hoofs on the second plane. But he can also consider the architecture of the base as a whole, with its magnificent receding geometrical motif above the coats of arms. Not only—as Salmi and Pittaluga observed—does the whole gain in monumentality, but both the equestrian group and the base are significantly placed in space. From a linear interpretation, this emphasizes the numerous silhouettes. Uccello was to adopt this conception with still greater intensity in the three panels of *The Battle of San Romano*.

Shortly after completing the portrait of *Sir John Hawkwood*, Uccello turned to the *Stories of the Holy Fathers* (plates 12–20), frescoed in the Cloister of San Miniato al Monte. The cycle, on two parallel walls in the *loggia* on the first floor, is mentioned in very early records; at some later date it was covered by plaster and mostly destroyed. Marangoni discovered fragments in 1925 and other pieces later came to light. Unfortunately, there are too few and too seriously damaged fragments to enable one to visualize the original effect without referring to Vasari's description of the whole cycle: "In San Miniato outside Florence, he did the cloister partly in *verde terra*, and partly in color, representing the lives of the Holy Fathers. But he did not observe a proper consistency in the use of his colors, for he made his fields blue, his city red, and his buildings of various hues according to his fancy. In this he was at fault, for buildings which are represented to be of stone cannot and ought not to be colored another tint." Vasari's words, even if critical, make one deeply regret such lost beauty! Those blue fields, red cities, and variously colored buildings "according to his fancy," must have been a source of joy to the beholder who, looking into the *loggia*, saw the walls stretching away. They were given life and expression by an architectural design consisting of a rhythmical succession of small, fluted columns, equidistant but never monotonous. The spaces between these columns are quite different from one another but all have a wonderfully suggestive perspective enhanced by the artist's "irrational" use of color.

It was the only way—or at least one of the best-planned artistic ways—to "interpret a wall" without falling back on cold ornamentation or treating it merely as a surface that has to be covered like some kind of huge, stiff scroll. It was a method which gave the wall aesthetic dimension, and its pictorial means were in keeping with the structure and surroundings. This partly explains the prevalence of architectural elements in the scenes, the emphasis placed on buildings rather than on human figures, which are few and scattered. The buildings, with their geometrical shapes, pointed corners, patches of different colors and sweep of perspective, strike the observer all together and before the individual stories. Because of their proximity to one another they suggest projections and depths in such a way that they animate the wall rhythmically and yet at the same time make one sense its unity. It is a method similar to that with which Uccello arranged groups of poles and lances in the three panels of *The Battle of San Romano* when the panels were linked in their original positions.

There is little more to say about the extraordinary landscapes in these *Stories*. "Blue fields" and barren, strangely shaped hills can be glimpsed between battlements, monastic cells with narrow rows of beautifully hewn stones, purple, yellow and red buildings, and pink and purplish paving-stones. Perhaps one can compare these landscapes with the background of the *St George and the Dragon* in the Musée Jacquemart-André in Paris (plate 21), executed at about this time. In this way one might avoid the temptation of comparing them with the almost suburban villages surrounded by Babylonian walls in Cimabue's well-known fresco in Assisi, or with the metaphysical "Italian piazzas" of early De Chirico works.

Parts of the figures in Uccello's San Miniato frescoes are still visible: monks, engulfed in their geometrically bell-shaped tunics (their solemn gestures are almost as stiff as those of paralytics), seated on stools outside the doors of their houses enjoying the last of the autumn sun; young boys with pots and pans; and perhaps loveliest of all, an angel (plate 17) whose head, as Marangoni said, "expresses all Uccello's artistic gospel." Marangoni also noticed that the angel's halo is not placed in the same perspective as the others—perhaps in order to make it harmonize better with the pure, calm face seen in profile and which, framed by the halo, is brought into relief by luminous contrast. This is, then, further proof of Uccello's free use of perspective and proof that his style was conscious. What is left of the figures on the south wall (Salmi rightly suspected the intervention of a collaborator) seems to be less severely outlined.

We see in the small *St George and the Dragon* (not a splendid work nor well preserved, but definitely attributed to Uccello) the same unity as in the landscapes of the *Stories of the Holy Fathers*. The figures might as easily represent nuns. Is the grave, massive St Monica flanked by two praying children a St Scholastica as Longhi thinks? This is a fragment of a destroyed work, now in the Contini-Bonacossi Collection in Florence (plate 33). St Monica belongs to a different religious Order, but the construction of the huge, imposing cloak, and the large, semicircular face bears a striking resemblance to the San Miniato monks. Her face should be compared with that of the monk (a little better preserved) who is portrayed full-face, seated in the fourth scene of the east wing in the Florentine cloister (plate 18). Framed by a large halo, she stands in purple-pink hues against an architectural background also outlined in perspective. This "discovery in coloring"—as Salmi points out—together with the "fine folds of her wimple," links her with the San Miniato frescoes. The lively children at her feet, their pure profiles and the light playing on their hair, are reminiscent of the beautiful angel (plate 19); and the minute folds of the sleeves, the raised arms of the child in the background bring to mind a fragment of a figure in the first scene in the south wing of the cloister (plate 20).

The attribution of the majestic figure of St Monica to Uccello (it has clear echoes of Masaccio's monumental art) is still strongly disputed—although Salmi and Pudelko attribute it definitely to Uccello. Above all, it has a bearing on whether or not another group of paintings is by Uccello. Neither Salmi nor Pudelko thinks that he executed the whole group.

This group, which Pope-Hennessy recently attributed to the Prato Master (Salmi prefers to ascribe works he does not believe to be by Uccello to the Master of the Quarata Predella), seems to me absolutely homogeneous—apart from the fact that the Prato frescoes reveal different stylistic qualities which could reasonably be explained by the participation of another artist. Uccello must have either executed all or none of the works that Pope-Hennessy attributed to the Prato Master. In addition to the *St Monica* they comprise: the *Virgin and Child* in the National Gallery, Dublin (plate 39); a predella in three parts with *The Adoration of the Magi* in the center (plates 40–41), *St John on Patmos* (plate 42) and *Two Kneeling Saints* (plate 43) on either side, in the Church of San Bartolommeo a Quarata, near Bagno a Ripoli; a predella depicting *The Dead Christ Between the Virgin and St John the Evangelist*, dated 1452, in Avane, near Florence (plate 60); scenes from the life of the Virgin and St Stephen in Prato Cathedral comprising *The Birth of the Virgin* (plate 24), *The Presentation of the Virgin in the Temple* (plate 25), and *The Dispute of St Stephen* (plate 26); and five single figures of saints at the entrance of the Chapel containing the previous scenes, *St Dominic* and *St Jerome* (plate 30), *St Paul* and *St Francis* (plate 31) and the *Blessed Jacopone da Todi* (plate 29) now in the Sacristy of the Cathedral. (I would certainly exclude the *Four Cardinal Virtues* on the roof of the Chapel, executed by another artist, and perhaps also the *St Dominic* and *St Paul* for its weak painting.) The three scenes are frescoed in the Capella dell'Assunta near the choir-stalls in the Cathedral. These frescoes can be clearly distinguished from the other frescoes in the Chapel which Sirèn suggested (1904) were executed by Andrea di Giusto. This is now unanimously accepted.

Of the works listed, those whose attribution to Uccello were most disputed are the frescoes by the Prato Master (plates 24–32). Now, in fact, only Longhi and Ragghianti attribute them to the Prato Master (previously Longhi believed them to be by Giovanni di Francesco del Cervelliera). The belief that the Prato frescoes were painted after 1445 had been largely responsible for making it difficult to accept them as Uccello's work. But Ragghianti has already pointed out that 1445 cannot be considered as a *terminus post quem*, for this date is connected with the renewing of the Chapel's glazed windows, and these could have been restored independently of the fresco execution; and after, more probably than before, the completion of the frescoes. The paintings may therefore be considered as of an earlier date. Moreover, the theory that *The Birth of the Virgin* could possibly derive from a similar scene frescoed by Domenico Veneziano, in the now lost series about St Egidius in Florence, does not seem to be correct. I am tempted to consider them as preceding chronologically even the San Miniato frescoes. Only in this way does their place in the evolution of Uccello's style— certainly not a consistent evolution—seem possible, even when the by now faint echoes of the Northern Late Gothic world reappear—the slender, preciously dressed women and the ornate objects in *The Birth of the Virgin*, the fantastic temple in the *Dispute of St Stephen*, the almost twentieth-century Venetian balustrade in *The Presentation of the Virgin in the Temple*—in fact, some of them have been attributed to Domenico Veneziano.

These are, perhaps, rather complex and even labored

speculations. Yet one should consider that particularly in these works the artist's inventiveness must have been linked far more closely—in subject-matter and purpose—with earlier iconographic traditions (with the exception of the stories from Genesis in the Chiostro Verde which are early works; an instance which was to be repeated later in the two circular windows in the cupola of the Church of Santa Maria del Fiore, plate 38). The theory that Uccello was influenced by Domenico Veneziano, to whom Schmarsow at first attributed the frescoes, has persisted. It would be better, perhaps, to reverse the attribution of one episode in the frescoes and speak of Uccello's influence on Veneziano. It may have been Veneziano's first experiment in Tuscany. Travelling from his native lagoon towards Umbria he might have stopped in Prato to greet his Florentine colleague whom he must either already have known or heard of in Venice.

This hypothesis is attractive, if admittedly somewhat too felicitous. It is perhaps more likely than the recent suggestion that Veneziano actually worked in Florence before his stay in Perugia in 1438. My view that these frescoes are the work of Veneziano is confirmed not only by an Uccellesque trend in Veneziano's first known works (clearly pointed out by Salmi) but also by a reaffirmation—although at second or third remove—of certain motifs from the frescoes of the Prato Master on a rough panel in Perugia, depicting the *Apocalyptic Lamb and the Madonna of the Misericordia* (especially the pious woman in profile kneeling at the Virgin's feet at right). Indeed, Salmi attributed this work to an Umbrian imitator of Veneziano. If my supposition could be more definitely proved one would certainly conclude that the frescoes of the Prato Master were already completed, or were being executed, around 1438. They testify to a cultural level which, from a Renaissance point of view, was still somewhat specious and "irrationally" involved very different elements: ranging from the lessons learned from the first Lippi—with traces of the meanest vernacular habits—to Bicci di Lorenzo and similar artists (for the moment Ghiberti is not brought into the matter).

Yet Uccello has the last word. His influence is decisive, even if not the most important. One recognizes it, indeed, in the spatial arrangement of the scenes no less than in the precise dimensions of the figures within the scenes—but for which the scenes are not expressly composed. Each participant is too absorbed in his own problem—which is to exist geometrically—to care about little else beyond the ground on which he stands, and beyond measuring himself against his neighbors and surroundings: so, while in *The Birth of the Virgin* the girl is a smaller edition of a woman, in *The Presentation of the Virgin in the Temple* the figures—even if perfectly proportioned—have become true dwarfs.

Exploiting the opportunities offered by perspective, especially in this last episode, belongs to a more genuine, more confident Uccello. The complicated carpentry of the Temple—the real protagonist of the scene—is built in a circular shape on three steps over a rectangular base from which the staircase leads; the whole structure is enclosed in a balustrade reduced to the most stereometric essentials. And again, the long line of hewn stones in the purple-red building at the left, from which the crystalline volume of a beam protrudes, is more than a reminder of perspective; it is an incisive element placed at that height for the purpose of setting off the vibrating, concise rhythm of the stairs (depicted in profile), the balustrade and the three-colored frieze on the Temple. In *The Birth of the Virgin* (plate 24) the bedchamber is placed high in the same way, and is slanted not only in order to animate the play of the geometric panels in the ceiling but also so that the altogether different perspective of the small staircase can develop under the arch of the lunette at the left. The similarities, particularly the facial resemblances, of these figures to subjects in other works known to be by Uccello has often been pointed out, especially to the last scenes in the Chiostro Verde (plates 44 and 53). This does not imply a derivation from the former to the latter but vice versa. For instance, young St John the Baptist's trembling, contrite face in the *Presentation of the Virgin in the Temple* (plate 25) anticipates the hollow masks of the *Prophets* on the clock-face at the west end of the Church of Santa Maria del Fiore, the Duomo (plates 34–37).

This is also true of the single figures of saints frescoed on the large arch at the entrance to the Capella dell' Assunta. Perhaps not to all of them, because at least two—*St Dominic* and *St Paul*—seem to have been retouched or completed by another artist. This unknown artist, however, has graphic characteristics different from the artist, perhaps of an earlier date, whose work appears in the *Four Cardinal Virtues* frescoed on the roof of the Chapel. The well-known *Blessed Jacopone da Todi*, and, more so, the *St Jerome* and *St Francis* with their huge profiles revolving in the semi-cylindrical alcoves of the niches, are certainly among the finest, most disciplined examples of Uccello's stylistic achievement at this period—an achievement in which there are reminders of the magnificent linear success of *Sir John Hawkwood*. The Sienese artists, Pietro and Giovanni Ambrosi, among others, were to draw inspiration from them even before 1444. The *St Bernardino* in Siena is reminiscent of the *St Francis*, in the circular sleeves of the frocks in both works and the open *incunabulum* of the *Blessed Jacopone da Todi*. This is further proof that the frescoes in Prato were executed before 1445.

Finally, the heads in the *clypei* (large oval shields) of the ornamental fascias which frame the scenes (plate 32) should be considered. Some are characterized by exceptional strength: the peasant wearing a *mazzocchio*, under *The Presentation of the Virgin in the Temple* (top figure, plate 32) recalls the drawing of the man in profile (bister wash on white paper) in the Uffizi (plate 117). This same strength can be seen in the young man portrayed full-face, the brim of his hat lined with squirrel fur (second figure left, plate 32). Other subjects reveal a subtle grace in the lines of their profiles: the young girl veiled in white to the right of *The Presentation of the Virgin in the Temple* (lower right figure, plate 32); or the almost romantic "severe vestal" (third figure right, plate 32) whose veil reminds one of the veil framing the beautiful Virgin in the *Virgin and Child* in Dublin (plate 39). This last is a masterpiece which—judging even from the photographic reproductions—must surely be by Uccello. For the painting is obviously composed to harmonize with the elliptical form and the sphere within the luminous niche (the work is attributed to Uccello by Pudelko and also by Salmi, though with some reservations). Its date, however—due precisely to the extreme formal discipline—must be rather later than the Prato frescoes; perhaps it immediately precedes Uccello's return to the Chiostro Verde (around 1450).

The numerous individual characterizations in the frescoes in Prato lead to a consideration of Uccello's portraits. There are various male portraits attributed to him—with the exception of the work depicting five founders of Florentine art (plate 62), in the Louvre, which will be dealt with later. All more or less recall the well-known *Portrait of a Gentleman* in Boston, attributed to Masaccio. However, the portrait that recent critics have almost unanimously attributed to Uccello is the *Portrait of a Young Man* (plate 121) in Chambéry. To me, this work does not seem substantially different from the two portraits of *Matteo Olivieri* and *Michele Olivieri* (plate 122), in Washington and New York respectively, which are usually ascribed to Domenico Veneziano.

A direct comparison of these three paintings might perhaps prove me wrong, especially since some parts of the small Chambéry portrait have been altered and repainted. I feel, however, that it would be splitting hairs to separate the Chambéry portrait from the other two which (although with reservations) can be said to be by Veneziano rather than by Uccello. In any case I think it unlikely that the Chambéry portrait is by Uccello—at any period of his activity. The work is excluded from his *œuvre* because of characteristics that are formal rather than physiognomical: the construction on very intensively modeled planes, the curve of the eyebrow lowered so that the eyebrow almost touches the bridge of the nose, and eye narrower and longer than is usual with Uccello. What decides the issue is a comparison with other similar subjects known to be by Uccello, and which should be chronologically close to these: the *Prophets* on the clock-face of Santa Maria del Fiore (plates 34–37), or the profile of Ham (plate 58) in *The Drunkenness of Noah* in the Chiostro Verde (that is, if one wishes to avoid comparison with the controversial Prato frescoes—the heads in the *clypei*, the young man at the right, assisting in *The Presentation of the Virgin in the Temple*).

The attribution of the "rectangular painting on wood" depicting five famous Florentine artists (plate 62), now in the Louvre, is more complicated. To begin with, the work is badly damaged and was repainted in the sixteenth century, which makes any consideration of the style difficult. In the sixteenth century the names inscribed under each figure were repainted (Giotto, Uccello, Donatello, Antonio Manetti, and

Brunelleschi). Although the identity of the characters is not certain, there is some possibility of comparing the ages of the figures in relation to their physical appearance (Giotto excluded, Brunelleschi and Donatello should appear older than Uccello, who was twenty years younger than Brunelleschi). In the first edition of his *Lives of the Artists* Vasari refers to a painting by Masaccio, depicting these five artists, as being in the home of the architect Giuliano da Sangallo. In the second edition he attributes the work to Uccello. A more likely theory is that these portraits might have derived from prototypes in fresco—one of which is the now lost *Saga of the Carmine* by Masaccio—but if one of the five figures is really Uccello then one cannot link Masaccio with this painting (nor with the lost work from which this would be a "late derivation with an honorary and commemorative purpose," as Ragghianti said). This is because Masaccio could not include Uccello among his distinguished friends and contemporaries, because the artist was in Venice at that time.

After consideration of these facts one still has the impression that the painting, though disfigured, was executed by Uccello in the period immediately preceding *The Battle of San Romano* panels. The work is little more than a memento; but an honorable and famous memento, not only because of the homage paid to the great artists but more because of the original composition and wonderful stylistic discipline, its solid forms powerfully outlined—particularly in the three-quarter-face portraits which must be among the earliest examples of "three-quarter figures painted in Tuscany under Flemish influence" (Salmi).

Critical controversy is quite strong about Uccello's female portraits. With the exception of those which have not been attributed to Uccello for a long time—for example, the portrait in the National Gallery, London (plate 128), now unanimously ascribed to Baldovinetti—three portraits of ladies in profile remain. They are respectively in the Metropolitan Museum of Art, New York (plate 23), in the Lehman Collection, New York (plate 126), and in the Gardner Museum, Boston (plate 127). After a preliminary attribution to Uccello, they were attributed by Offner to the so-called Master of the Castello "Nativity." It is an attribution which enjoyed and still seems to be enjoying limited success, and is confirmed in Pope-Hennessy's monograph on Uccello. Pudelko attributes two of the portraits to the Master of the Karlsruhe "Adoration," an artist different from both Uccello and the Master of the Castello "Nativity." I consider that Salmi is right in shrewdly distinguishing the portrait in the Metropolitan Museum of Art from the other two; it is similar to the Boston portrait only in appearance (but to such an extent that Pittaluga accidentally reproduced the Boston portrait instead of the Metropolitan one). Salmi strongly defends the attribution of the Metropolitan portrait to Uccello.

This portrait is undoubtedly a masterpiece and one of the most sublime examples of Uccello's stylistic coherence. Critics have highly praised this anonymous aristocratic lady, quite apart from who they believed the artist was. But in this portrait of such an integrated profile, one should at this point note how the image is defined with no signs of hesitancy, breaks or projections; it is reduced to its most geometrical essentials while miraculously preserving features that are smooth, pliant and graceful (a very difficult balance which not even the painter of the magnificent portrait in Boston— if he is indeed Domenico Veneziano—achieved, probably because he was concentrating on quite different aspects). The Metropolitan portrait has as its closest equivalent the girl with the white veil (plate 32) in the Prato frescoes.

Therefore this portrait should be dated not long after the Prato cycle.

The superb articulation of the *Portrait of a Lady* (plate 23) was not to be equaled even when Uccello portrayed authentic princesses as in the two *St George and the Dragon* paintings, one in the Musée Jacquemart-André in Paris (plate 21) and the other in the National Gallery, London (plate 66).

They are compositions that are attractive rather than stylistically valid. This applies particularly to the Paris version, which is contemporary with or very close to the San Miniato frescoes (taking into account the repainting which seriously affects the work). It is a small *cassone* (marriage chest) panel, depicting three figures in a line in the foreground in front of a cave which, like Saladin's tent, uselessly clutters the landscape. The perspective of the landscape is directed upward, the fields are patterned like a chess board (a Lorenzetti touch), there is a towered city in the background, and three small figures—one in a vivid, beautiful red—stroll peacefully along a wide deserted avenue. These elements are perhaps the only poetic features of the painting. The landscape is not linked in any way with the figures—even if the ridiculous dragon vainly attempts to "insert himself into space" by means of his spiraling, corkscrew tail. Of very different calibre is the *St George and the Dragon* in London. Chronologically the work is later, if one considers (as does Boeck) that the huge, muscular rearing horse (plate 67) is more Baroque than the horses in the panels of *The Battle of San Romano*, and has echoes of the horse in Andrea del Castagno's *St Nicholas of Tolentino* (1456). Rider and dragon are dexterously placed across the picture space in a diagonal perspective between the cave and the pine forest, stretching as far as the distant mountain range;

they form a kind of ideal cone with its apex at the dragon's jaws, which seem to echo the gaping entrance to the cave. The composition is filled with movement, and the head of the princess on its long neck is stamped against the dark background of the cave with the same sharp prominence as the riders in the *Hunt by Night* at Oxford (plates 100–101).

Of secondary importance in the development of Uccello's style are the two large circular stained-glass windows depicting *The Nativity* and the *Resurrection* in the cupola of the Church of Santa Maria del Fiore (plate 38). In 1443–44 the artist executed three cartoons for different windows; the third, representing *The Ascension*, was rejected. Certainly some of the original concept has been modified and lost in the translation into glass. We clearly see a partial return to Ghibertian forms in the surviving windows—regardless of the numerous perspective elements—due, perhaps, to the fact that Ghiberti was then the principal supplier of cartoons for the Cathedral's windows and Uccello did not want to stray too far from his first master's style. *The Nativity* is mediocre and laboriously composed, but *The Resurrection* is rescued by the magnificent image of Christ, whose aery curved lines contrast with the severe setting of the sepulcher in the background, and with the shrunken figures of the sleeping soldiers on each side. There is a very different strength in the four *Prophets* (plates 34–37) with which, in 1443 (Ragghianti thinks 1437), Uccello decorated the corners of the clock-face in Santa Maria del Fiore.

Here, too, the theme is Ghibertian and was possibly suggested by the small projecting heads in Ghiberti's *Door of Paradise*. Yet at this time the artists most influencing Uccello were Masaccio and Donatello. Uccello had already approximated Masaccio, taking some suggestions from figures in the predella of Masaccio's Carmine Altarpiece in

Pisa (not in Berlin) for his *Adoration of the Magi* in the predella in the Church of San Bartolommeo a Quarata (plates 40–41). But he limited himself to individual iconographic elements (the Virgin and Child, the kneeling king, the donkey's pack-saddle) without any attempt to conform to the substance of Masaccio's style. The intensely compressed monumentality of the Berlin predella is dissolved here into an elegant rhythm (still in Late Gothic taste) in the small ethereal scene which is dominated by the fragile open framework of the hut, together with the crystalline pyramid of the tent and the clear-cut outlines of the spirited little horse outlined against a mysterious forest at night. On the clock-face of Santa Maria del Fiore, however, the attempt at a chiefly plastic language is felt not only in the massive, unified structure of the heads which project almost laboriously from the apertures (whose circular frames stand out clearly from the background), but also in the light which envelops and severely models the tormented features. These are rendered with a great strength reminiscent of Andrea del Castagno. The strange feverish pathos tormenting and consuming the gloomy executioner-like features makes them similar to the Donatello statues in Giotto's Campanile. But they do not, however, attain the spiritual grandeur of the statues: the stern Uccello *Prophets* contain a remnant of cold discipline which is revealed even in the peaceful play of the haloes against the moon-like curves of the perspectively rendered circular apertures—despite the much more literal rendering of some elements (Masaccio, e.g., had portrayed the curly hair of an Apostle in *The Tribute Money* with different strength).

The series of *Giants* in chiaroscuro which Uccello executed two years later, in 1445, in the courtyard of the Casa Vitaliani in Padua, could not have been very different in style and spirit from the *Prophets* in Santa Maria del Fiore—

if, as Vasari says, they "were greatly admired by Andrea Mantegna." The cycle was destroyed a long time ago and only recently—mostly due to Ragghianti's research—have critics managed to reconstruct the aspects which would have most interested young Mantegna.

Other possible evidence of Uccello's stay in the Veneto has been pointed out by Fiocco and Salmi. The most important evidence can be seen in the architecture of the *Visitation* and *The Presentation of the Virgin in the Temple*, executed in mosaic (the figures are by Giambono) in the Capella Mascoli in St Mark's in Venice. Pudelko and Longhi attribute these mosaic structures directly to Uccello, while Salmi believes they were renewed around 1454 by Jacopo Bellini, who must have recalled Uccello's now lost frescoes in Vitaliani's house. However, Uccello could not have stayed long in the Veneto. He went on to Padua, summoned, as Vasari says, by Donatello in 1445; and in 1447 he must have been back in Florence. Contrary to what happened on Uccello's first stay away from home, this second journey, made when he was much more mature and consequently in a position to leave his own mark on the artistic trends of every region he visited, failed to enrich his figurative work with any further Venetian influences, and instead led him—undoubtedly because of the constant company of his friend Donatello—into a new and reinvigorating area: the art of Tuscany.

The works Uccello executed in Florence shortly after his return from the Veneto are proof of this: they are the two scenes representing *The Flood and The Recession of the Flood* (plate 44), and *The Sacrifice of Noah and The Drunkenness of Noah* (plate 53), frescoed around 1450 in the Chiostro Verde of Santa Maria Novella. Most probably—and Pope-Hennessy agrees—the perspective procedure of *The Flood* was suggested by Donatello's relief of *The Miracle of the Penitent Son* for the Church of Sant'Antonio in Padua which was completed by 1447.

But even if the two compositions are superficially similar, the resulting styles and poetry are profoundly different. In the magnificent Donatello relief, the vast luminous space, defined by the buildings and stairs in perspective, gravitates toward the central episode (the young man is lying in the mathematical center of the composition in the foreground; a center which is stressed higher up by the corner of the building in the background). Space constitutes the limits of the miracle; it magnifies and spreads its psychological effect among the crowd and is responsible for the solemnity of the event. It is in fact because of Uccello's handling of space that the impersonal crowd acquires a physiognomy and character that is not degraded by baser individual figures. The spectators are mainly placed in groups but each is united with all the others around the young man; they "use" the architectural elements by going up and down the stairs, gathering in the shadows, peering over the balustrades. The empty space which one imagines is behind the figures placed like a screen around the miracle is necessary to make one feel the unusualness of the event. It is not empty space as such, but a space suddenly emptied of its former occupants who are running toward the foreground. It seems still to be vibrating from the running feet and reflects the anxiety of the tiny figures who have remained in the background staring over the balustrades.

To this wonderful unity of vision and power of synthesis, Uccello contrasts (always within the numerous episodes with which he realizes his concept of the event) a principle of unity that is just as valid: his figurative coherence. It is necessary here to repeat that Uccello looks through individual entities; that they interest him in so far as they can be represented according to predetermined criteria of regularity, outline, plasticity and linear "eloquence," which are far removed from, and even opposed to mere decoration. These criteria are carried out in the intense volumes of each figure, a self-enclosed entity, as much as in the severely geometrical forms of the objects—like the floating ladder and cask, and the two arks; they are also controlled (but not as a necessary consequence) by spatial dimensions determined by the relation between the two arks and their vanishing point in the background.

I do not want to use the term "abstract," which is always misleading. Nor do I want to affirm—as many have done—that Uccello was indifferent to the tragedy inherent in this subject. Vasari has been criticized for his description of *The Flood* (see comment on plate 44). One cannot criticize him for not judging by present critical standards, but I am tempted to give him credit. Although damaged, the fresco continues to suggest a sinister, terrifying cosmic cataclysm by means of its somber, grayish colors, cruelly stressed by vivid light which contrasts with reddish shadows. The drowning figures, their frantic gestures, and the pitiful remains of a devastated world seem to be activated by the same anguish that is inherent in the space in which the chaotic event takes place. We can distinguish and isolate all these figures much as the artist saw them in his initial concept, and each forces the observer to participate in the drama. One's eye runs easily along the twin perspectives of the arks and so on to the more distant scenes: the oak tree split by lightning; the naked man fleeing (upper left, plate 46) and displaying the same fantastic intensity as the woman near the cask (lower foreground, plate 50) and the two men fighting in the foreground (lower left, plate 44). This tormented, almost nightmarish simultaneity which is revealed by all the scenes and aspects of the event has that inherent spatial dimension which I mentioned earlier. It also provides Uccello with a great opportunity to express lyrically the tragic significance of the catastrophe.

The figure of Noah praying (plate 46) more than dominates all other figures. It is abstracted from them in a way that seems to make him stand out and away from the fabric of the composition. Noah is, as Salmi pointed out, rendered very differently from the others: he is freely and stereometrically conceived and the luminous thick wool robes and wrinkled face have rich pictorial substance (plate 47). His serenity towers above the tumult of the dying and drowned bodies, giving evidence of unshaken faith in God. Masaccio's generous inspiration is present here, still far from dormant some twenty-five years later.

Echoes of Masaccio are also present in the fresco beneath *The Flood*: it consists of two scenes which are linked a little spuriously by a vine-covered trellis executed in perspective. The scenes are *The Sacrifice of Noah and The Drunkenness of Noah* (plate 53). The fresco is in a very bad state and about one-third of the lower part has completely vanished. But the solemnity of the occasion is still evident in the grave crowd surrounding the Ark: serious, cloaked figures, they recall—especially the beautiful back view of a woman—Masaccio's figures. Their faces are absorbed and filled with inner sweetness—for instance, Noah, with his eyes raised to the sky and the image of God above (plate 54), represented with bold foreshortening (which Vasari greatly admired). Uccello gave perhaps an over-calculated and too obvious display of his virtuosity in perspective.

Despite the help of ancient engravings, it is less easy to

comment on *The Drunkenness of Noah*. The fallen figure of the Patriarch, which must also have been rendered with daring foreshortening, has disappeared. The barrel, too, is gone (its perspective was criticized by Vasari). The monumental figures of the three children remain as imposing figures in the wreck of the hut: Ham who appears in profile (plate 58) was, according to tradition, supposed to represent the Florentine painter, Dello Delli, who at the time had just returned from Spain; the circular head of Shem is framed by a *mazzocchio* (plate 59); and Japhet (right, plate 57) compassionately averts his eyes from his father's nakedness—his great curved back is of the magnificence of some of Luca Signorelli's figures.

Not long after these frescoes in the Chiostro Verde were completed Uccello executed a fresco of *The Nativity and the Annunciation to the Shepherds* (plate 61) in a lunette in the ex-Hospital of San Martino alla Scala. The fresco was discovered in 1934 when it was already reduced to a shadow and there are no early engravings to enable any kind of accurate reconstruction of the composition. It is therefore impossible to establish whether it is an autograph work or (as Salmi supposes) whether Uccello merely executed the outlines and left the completion to an inexperienced assistant. I have already pointed out the unusual perspective with its two separate vanishing points; from the scanty remains it is still possible to assume this logically. But we are also forced to imagine the resulting lyrical effect. This must have almost produced a sense of vertigo in the limitless space fanning magically outward, filled with the rectangular pattern of numerous fields and the flagstones of the stable, and unified by the figure of the Virgin in the foreground.

The three famous panels of *The Battle of San Romano*

(plates 68–69, 80–81 and 92–93) were, according to popular tradition, executed between 1456 and 1460. In 1456—as Salmi notes—in honor of their leader, the *condottiere* Niccolò Maurucci da Tolentino, the Florentines commissioned an equestrian portrait of him from Andrea del Castagno (now in the Duomo)—in the same way as twenty years earlier they had commissioned *Sir John Hawkwood* from Uccello. The three panels, against a backing of cypresses, were placed at one end of a ground-floor room in the Palazzo Medici in Via Larga. They commemorate a Florentine victory in which Niccolò da Tolentino routed the Sienese troops. The battle took place on June 1, 1432 in the neighborhood of San Romano. The leader of the Sienese troops was Bernardino della Ciarda who had once been in the service of the Florentines but was now in alliance with the Dukes of Milan.

The first panel, on the left (National Gallery, London, plates 68–69), represents Niccolò and his knights charging the Sienese. Beneath a banner with a device of knots around a scorpion (plate 79) he rides a rearing white horse and carries a commander's baton (plate 70). He is dressed for battle with a short cloak over his armor; beneath a huge red and gold brocade hat his face is clean-shaven. A fair-haired page on horseback follows, carrying his helmet (plate 72). The battle is already fully engaged. In fact, Niccolò, accompanied by not more than twenty horsemen, had resisted the Sienese attack for eight hours. The ground about him is littered with pieces of armor, shattered lances, a helmet (plate 76) and the body of an armed knight lying on his face (plate 77). At the extreme left, trumpeters sound their instruments (plate 74) under a group of lances. The scene is contained in the background by a thick green hedge dotted with oranges and roses; behind this rises a barren hill, its slopes scattered with knights and foot-soldiers (plate 78).

At the right of the center panel and balancing the London scene was the panel depicting the second stage of the battle (Louvre, plates 92–93): the arrival of Florentine reinforcements under Micheletto Attendolo da Cotignola. He is on a black horse (plate 98); above his impressive brocade hat (plate 99) is a banner bearing a unicorn, and around flutter other banners with black and silver bands (plate 98). Since the attack is not yet under way, the ground is still clear. A group of knights wait patiently at his right (plate 96), but other horsemen and infantry (left) who are in the rear are already rushing forward.

The center panel (Uffizi, plates 80–81) represents the conclusion of the battle. Bernardino della Ciarda is unhorsed by the impact of a lance hurled by an enemy horseman (plate 82). He is depicted in a confused crowd of armed horsemen and infantry, from which lances, spears, poles and crossbows project. The whole scene is cluttered with horses, soldiers and fallen arms.

The scenes represented in the three panels are not synchronized; both the lack of continuity in the landscapes and the distribution of the figures prevent the panels from being considered as a single composition. Uccello took into account the complex effect they would have created beside one another on the same wall, and perhaps calculated their sequence and the space to be left between them. Framed and yet separated by the groups of lances and poles, the three scenes converge toward the foreground of the center panel.

Here, contrasting with the extremely dense crowd of foreshortened figures, the great white horse of Bernardino della Ciarda is represented in full profile. Its mass is rendered as horizontal as possible and its outlines become more majestically impressive as they become more geometrically absolute. The studied rhythmic and color relations between the three panels (as, for example, Niccolò's white horse followed by a group of dark horses in the left panel which is balanced by Micheletto's dark horse followed by a group of light horses in the right panel), the sequence of dense and thin crowds of fighters stressed by the different angles of the groups of poles, unite these three episodes, separated in time. It has therefore an exclusively visual simultaneity (which is metaphorically logical and legitimate) and has no need to resort to naturalistic means (as would have been the case had the artist placed the episodes within a continuous landscape, probably separated by groups of rocks, trees, or other such elements).

Space in the three panels is, then, real—a concrete fact that one can actually see in its unity and formal discipline. Yet it is a space which has a "logic" other than the spatial logic of nature. It is a space which has the same form as the horses who are not "real" horses; as the armor, plumes and flaming crests of the helmets; a space generated by the same expressive aspirations, the same fantastic impetus that transfigured the horses or revealed the shining intrinsic beauty of the forms of other ordinary objects.

Horses, riders, armor are seen in perspective. But Uccello's perspective is disconnected and limited to individual objects. In the Uffizi panel the perspective of each horse is different from its neighbor. Yet it is precisely this infinite variety in perspective that constitutes one of the major characteristics of Uccello's art. One is to all intents proving how faithful he was to his own inspiration when one repeats that experiments in perspective were, for him, nothing more than the means to realize values absolutely independent of the illusionary or naturalistic values inherent in mathematical theory. Uccello represents horses or any fragment of reality that may form part of his vision in an image that is highly consistent with his ideal of formal and chromatic absoluteness. The function of color, too, is very important in his work; one can best see this in the London panel, which has preserved the fine tones and their unexpected and daring interrelationships, which because of their new reaction to light are very different from Gothic chromatism. The artist studied or carefully considered every viewpoint, every possible arrangement in an ideal space—in which, indeed, everything has a place, and in which he drew "profiles" of profound aesthetic significance.

The spiritual tension (one could even call it ecstasy) of this study, this re-creation of the data of perceptible reality, reveals no trace of hesitancy or weariness—at least in the panels of *The Battle of San Romano* and *The Flood*. And, as in *The Flood*, the result is far from being merely a story or a refined stylistic exercise; it is not the product of "insatiable ingenuity" or "childlike fickleness" which "transforms everything into a game—fantasy rather than thought." The result—according to my own impressions—is the conscious reaction of a sensitive temperament, humane and imaginative, confronted with the terrifying and yet, in its own way, fascinating reality of war: a fierce, anonymous battle between two sides that have become the instruments of blind destiny.

War and battles have inspired countless numbers of great artists: from the artist of the mosaic *Battle of Isso* to Picasso. Uccello figures among them. He did not confine himself to representing the most picturesque outward aspects, nor did he portray the physical horror and torment of war. Nor, again, did he exalt the moral element which, paradoxically, produces strength of character, such as courage and stoicism. Using his imagination, Uccello relived the concrete, physically limited action between two groups of armed contemporaries—he had certainly seen them during military expeditions, parades or tournaments. And he must have experienced a fascination that was accompanied by an indefinable sense of anguish on seeing the mighty apparatus which can transform a human being into a fighter: the tightly closed, glinting suits of armor, the terrible visors, gauntlets, cumbersome poles, the brazen plumed crests and banners, the huge swords and trumpets, the lances, crossbows and the muscular, richly harnessed horses, their animal vitality ready to be unleashed. It was an array of a huge armory, and its threatening aspect is evoked with nightmarish precision; it carries with it a scent of old leather, of helmets, oiled metal and horseflesh. These inanimate menacing objects are incited to overwhelm one another by some kind of transcendent occult force. They charge, collide, are repulsed; they push, stumble, ride over one another, become hopelessly entangled; they are cut in two, they fall. Forms seem to magnify in the confusion and uproar: horses become machines, men are transformed into automatons and terrifying robots. Is all this merely fantasy or a story?

One would not experience this vivid sensation of being part of a nightmare if the artist had not transfigured reality so completely, and if he had not managed to imprison the observer in the magic circle of his imagination. If, for instance, he had placed the figures and horses in a purely perspective space or if he had related their positions more "realistically," perhaps they would then have seemed more like puppets and rocking-horses. The "unreal" space strengthens the observer's conviction about their forms; and their "unreal" form gives lyrical expression to their "improbable" movements and positions. In the Uffizi panel the action of the famous kicking horse (plate 83) is—without knowing anything about horses—clearly organically incorrect, absurd and probably quite impossible. Yet the kicking rendered by Uccello's method is more terrifying and has more impact than the kicking of a horse in real life! This also applies to the duel fought between the knights to the right of Niccolò da Tolentino in the London panel (plate 71). The cumbersome movements of the figures and their horses suggest a fatal intensity which is tragic. One can see it, too, in the magnificent horizontally placed scene in which the Sienese leader is thrown off his mount (plates 82 and 84). The violent crash of his fall seems more irrevocable because the rigid perspective volumes of his armor unbalance the spatial position of the horse in full profile. The fury with which Cotignola's cavalry attacks (plate 94) is emphasized by the poles and lances, inclined in a horizontal, almost fan-like direction with the plumed crests pointing the opposite way. One can see it, finally, in the somber sense of expectation that surrounds the knights and the closely packed heads of their horses in the platoon behind Cotignola (plate 95).

I do not want to force my interpretation of these famous compositions to the extent of attributing obscure metaphysical meanings to them. Nor should one consider Uccello, fascinated as he was with the wonderful equipment of the contemporary militia, as being merely concerned with expressing their fierceness in action. At the same time, he was not a philosopher contemplating the fatality and blind stupidity of war that reduces man and beast to puppets; possibly no one considered these things at that time. Yet one is none the less aware of how the artist's imagery and daring style, with all its mature, conscious and impassioned sincerity, managed to express the terrifying eruption of conflict as successfully as he had expressed earlier the

Biblical tragedy of *The Flood*—although here the event is tougher, less easily accepted and critically less "elegant" than that which involved the irresponsible dreamer, the weaver of colored tales.

One can also admit that one has been deceived. But to anyone who criticizes me for being too ingenious, I can reply that there is still some truth in the old, almost discredited story about the famous aria in Gluck's opera, *Orpheus*. If the lines, "*J'ai perdu mon Eurydice—rien n'égale mon malheur*," are sung "*J'ai trouvé mon Eurydice—rien n'égale mon bonheur*," the result is still a masterpiece.

The works Uccello executed after the panels of *The Battle of San Romano* can add little more to his stature. Indeed, they are but further proof of his stylistic ability. Now aging and representative of a rather outdated fashion, the artist was probably forced mainly to paint "pictures in perspective for couches, beds and other small articles," and he had to resign himself to producing more commercial works. But as far as one knows he never surrendered his artistic dignity in executing these minor commissions. Proof of this is a scene representing a *Hunt by Night* (plates 100–101) in the Ashmolean Museum, Oxford, which may have decorated a *cassone*. It is still called a hunt "by night" because of the crescent moon, now barely visible in the foliage (plate 103)— although Lionello Venturi cleverly observes that in reality, "night doesn't figure at all, and if this is natural light it is of an extra-terrestrial nature—of the planet fantasy." Historically, Venturi explains, it is a "freeing of the juxtaposition of colors not as a result of light and shade ... but as a result of the paradoxical contrast of intense colors." It is interesting to note how often the rising moon appears in Uccello's works: so much so, that in a recent very "Parisian" review he was described, semi-esoterically and semi-surrealistically, as a "*peintre lunaire.*"

The enchanting *Hunt by Night*—some stylistic characteristics in foliage and undergrowth recall the Quarata Predella—must have been executed soon after the panels of *The Battle of San Romano*. The agile greyhounds (plates 102–104) are related to the nimble hares bounding across the hills of the Uffizi battle scene (plates 90–91). Their foreshortened positions accentuate the vitality expressed, not by the vibrating contours, but by the taut elasticity of the curved sharp profiles against the dark green forest. The scene takes place, this time, within a single spatial perspective but it seems divided by the arrangement of the graded tree-trunks which greatly intensify the swarming little figures which gradually diminish until both humans and animals become microscopic. The whole scene is rendered with fantastic clarity and brilliant colors. It suggests a kind of game of roulette on a green carpet, dotted with unusual plants and flowers; black rotted pine trunks protrude in perspective, like spikes of a wheel; purple reflections are thrown from a near-by pond fringed with the sharp stems of bulrushes (lower foreground, plates 102–103). Hunters and beaters wearing flame-colored short cloaks, red-harnessed horses, dogs and game, all suddenly seem to be frozen in elegant poses, acquiring the studied refinement of heraldic symbols —not without a touch of witticism and gentle irony, though, that is revealed in the hunters' pointed noses, small gaping mouths and emphatic movements (which led Pope-Hennessy to suspect the influence of some Flemish or French prototype).

The element of caricature in the features, containing a very natural Expressionism, is to be found in two other paintings which were probably Uccello's last works: the small panel representing *Christ on the Cross with the Virgin and SS John the Baptist, John the Evangelist and Francis* (plate 114) in the Thyssen Collection, Lugano; and the predella representing *The Profanation of the Host* (plates 106–108) in Urbino.

The first of these two works is controversial. Above all, the date of its execution is very uncertain. But the dryness of the formal language, its clear, concise volumes, the insistence on perspective, and even the severity of the inspiration, do not support an attribution to the Master of the Karlsruhe "Adoration" (whose name comes from a charming work, flowery and richly decorative, now at Karlsruhe). One can suppose the date was around 1420; the often-noticed similarities with the *Hunt by Night* (the profile of the weeping St John) and with the Urbino Predella are very strong.

The second work is documented and can be dated with certainty. It was commissioned by the Company of Corpus Domini of Urbino as a predella to stand under an altarpiece. Piero della Francesca refused the commission for the altarpiece, and it was eventually given to a Flemish artist, Justus of Ghent. Uccello received payment for the predella between February 6, 1467 and October 17, 1469 in the form of clothes as well as money. He completed it, indeed, when he was over seventy years old. One is therefore tempted to wonder if his artistic abilities were now in decline and whether Vasari was right in saying that Uccello's work worsened as he aged.

The excellence of the predella contradicts this. In spite of its small dimensions, the story of the sacrilege is told with untroubled concentration and with no evidence of complacency. There are no suggestions of a return to the still delightful "ingenuities" of the fourteenth century. There is,

44

indeed, a sense of full participation, and space and color are united in a synthesis that is stylistically severe but filled with a new inventive felicity.

The background consists of brown hills scattered with fruit-laden trees and cottages glimpsed in the distance. The continuity is interrupted only at the right of the second scene, in which the episode is transferred to the interior of the house and shop. Against this background the figures are placed with sureness and clarity. There are six episodes, each perfectly conclusive and proportioned, separated by a spacious succession of elegantly designed vermilion pilasters. The depth of the perspective, particularly stressed in the first two scenes by the diverging lines of the ceiling beams and the rectangular tiles on the floors, is rendered with a highly dramatic effect. In the first scene, the bare wall bathed in light and the geometrically shaped fireplace crowned with shields are mute witnesses to the action taking place between the man and the woman in a dark cloak; the tiny Host is silhouetted against a black book on the counter between them. In the second scene the foreshortened wall, again bare and fully lit, stresses the horror of the man and his family as they watch a stream of blood pour from the Host. Outside, a group of soldiers are forcing open the door of the sacrilegious house. These are the two most intense scenes and are rightly the best known. But the others are almost as effective: the grave procession in which the Pope replaces the Host on the altar; the execution of the woman who turns repentant eyes to the intervening angel descending from the sky, watched by stupefied soldiers; the fire which reflects vivid colors on the clothes of the burning unbeliever and his family; and even the last scene, in which angels and devils argue over the woman's corpse, could not have been rendered with more simplicity and economy of means. The enchanting, jewel-like colors are distributed everywhere and reveal keen perception in the way they are used to render objects close or distant. Each object and each figure acquires a miraculous new aspect by means of color.

"In this pure, effervescent fervor, all problems which bothered the artist elsewhere are now resolved. Each problem is simplified, or better still, finds its own solution. The need for essentials, which stemmed from his innermost being, is here completely and immediately answered" (Mary Pittaluga). The year he completed the Urbino Predella Uccello declared: "I find myself old and ailing, my wife is ill and I can no longer work." He lived six more years and at the age of seventy-eight, on December 10, 1475, death liberated him from misery and from obscurity.

BIOGRAPHICAL NOTES

1397. Uccello born in Florence. Father: Dono di Paolo, barber and surgeon of Pratovecchio (a Florentine citizen from 1373). Mother: Antonia di Giovanni Castello del Beccuto.

1407, JUNE 1. His name is included in a list of workmen employed by Ghiberti. Listed as an "errand boy" at a wage of five florins a year. A few years later (around 1412) his wage is shown as twenty-five florins a year.

1415, OCTOBER 15. He is registered at the Guild of Florence as Apothecary and Surgeon. Lives in the parish of Santa Maria Nepoticosa.

1424. Listed as a member of the Painters Company of San Luca.

1425, AUGUST 5. Makes a will in which he leaves everything to the Hospital of Santa Maria Nuova, and gives instructions that he is to be buried in his father's tomb in the Church of Santo Spirito. Lives in the parish of Santa Maria Novella.

1425–30 (c.). At Venice, where his presence is recorded in 1427. Works on mosaics for St Mark's.

1431. Returns to Florence.

1431, JANUARY 31. Declares his personal properties to the Tax Office in Florence.

1432. Asks to be employed in the Church of Santa Maria del Fiore.

On March 23, the Office of Works writes to Pietro Beccanugi, Florentine Ambassador in the Venetian Republic, to ask for information about Uccello's ability as an artist in mosaic.

1436, MAY 30. First commission for *Sir John Hawkwood*. Second commission July 6. Payment for this fresco made on August 31.

1442. Pays revenue to the Tax Office in Florence.

1443, FEBRUARY–1445, JANUARY 28. Various commitments for the cartoons for the large stained-glass windows in the Church of Santa Maria del Fiore.

1443. Documents relating to the completion of the *Prophets* on the clock-face of the Church of Santa Maria del Fiore.

1445. Journeys to Padua, summoned by Donatello.

1446. Returns to Florence. A record in the Tax Office notes that he lives in the Via della Scala near the Church of Santa Maria d'Ognissanti, and has a shop in the Piazza San Giovanni.

1450. Receives payment for the painting of a tabernacle in the Church of San Giovanni.

1451, FEBRUARY 22. Presents a petition to the Guild of Calimale.

1451, MARCH 13. Gives an estimate for a tabernacle painted by Stefano d'Antonio.

1453. Birth of a son, Donato.

1453, JUNE 30. Receives payment for a fresco representing the Blessed Andrea Corsini in the Library of Santa Maria del Fiore.

1456. Joins in partnership with the master glazier, Bernardo di Francesco, for the purpose of executing two cartoons for two large stained-glass windows in Santa Maria del Fiore.

1456. Birth of his daughter, Antonia.

1457, FEBRUARY 15. Declaration to Tax Office.

1465. In Urbino with his son, Donato, to discuss the terms for a predella of an altarpiece for the main altar.

1467, FEBRUARY 6–1469, OCTOBER 17. Receives payments for the predella at Urbino.

1469, AUGUST 8. In a declaration to the Tax Office he writes: "I find myself old and ailing, my wife is ill, and I can no longer work."

1475, NOVEMBER 11. Makes a will.

1475, DECEMBER 10. Dies (the *Anonimo Gaddiano* states that he died in hospital) and is buried in his father's tomb in the Church of Santo Spirito.

UCCELLO'S PAINTINGS

Plate 1

THE CREATION OF THE ANIMALS and THE CREATION OF ADAM; THE CREATION OF EVE and THE FALL. *Frescoes, 210 × 452; and 244 × 478.** Florence, Convent of Santa Maria Novella, Chiostro Verde (first extension of east wing).* Mentioned as Uccello's work by earliest records (among them Antonio Manetti, Francesco Albertini, the *Libro di Antonio Billi* and the *Codice Magliabechiano*). Vasari writes: "He was afterwards allotted some scenes in the cloister of Santa Maria Novella. The first of these are where one enters the church from the cloister, and represents the creation of the animals with an infinite number of different creatures, fishes, beasts and birds. And because he was very fanciful and, as I have said, took great delight in making animals well, he showed his pride in some lions about to fall on one another with open jaws, and the fleetness and timidity of certain stags and bucks. Birds and fishes are painted with the greatest exactitude in every feather and scale. Here also he painted the creation of man and of woman, with their sin, in a beautiful style, carefully and finely executed. And in this work he took pleasure in the coloring of the trees, which had not usually been well done up to that time."

The attribution of these frescoes to Uccello has been accepted by almost all modern critics, with the exception only of Longhi and Fiocco who believe them to be by Dello Delli. Van Marle attributed them to one of Uccello's pupils, and Boeck excludes them from Uccello's œuvre. They are generally dated soon after the artist's return from Venice (1430) and before the completion of the equestrian portrait of *Sir John Hawkwood* (1436). Only Horne suggests they may have been completed before Uccello's departure for Venice (1425). The frescoes are mostly executed in *terra verde*, with dark red backgrounds and very few traces of other colors. As they were seriously damaged, they were removed from the wall in 1940 by the Central Institute of Restoration and this process brought to light the underlying cartoons, which enabled a reconstruction of the composition of some parts of the lower scenes which had been destroyed. (See also plates 2–9. For Uccello's other frescoes in the Chiostro Verde see plates 44–59.)

Plate 2

THE CREATION OF THE ANIMALS. See commentary on plates 1, 4 and 5.

Plate 3

THE CREATION OF ADAM. See commentary on plates 1 and 6.

* All dimensions are given in centimeters.

Plate 4

THE CREATION OF THE ANIMALS.
Detail: animals.

Plate 5

THE CREATION OF THE ANIMALS.
Detail: God the Father.

Plate 6

THE CREATION OF ADAM. Detail:
head of Adam.

Plate 7

THE CREATION OF EVE. See
commentary on plate 1.

Plate 8

THE FALL. See commentary on
plate 1.

Plate 9

THE FALL. Detail: female head of
the serpent.

Plate 10

SIR JOHN HAWKWOOD, KNOWN
AS GIOVANNI ACUTO. *Fresco, 820
× 515. Florence, Duomo.* The Florentines decided to honor the English
leader, Sir John Hawkwood, who
led the Florentine troops to victory
in the Battle of Cascina (July 28,
1364), while he was still living, by
erecting a tomb in the Duomo *"in
qua posit recondi corpus ipsius domini
Johannis quando morietur"* (1393).
Hawkwood died in 1394. It was then
agreed that monuments to both
Hawkwood and the *condottiere*
Piero Farnese should be erected. The
Hawkwood monument was not in
marble, as originally planned, but
took the form of a fresco executed by
Agnolo Gaddi and Giuliano d'Arrigo
in 1395. On May 30, 1436, Uccello
was instructed to replace the existing
fresco but on July 6, 1436 was
instructed to make a second attempt
as his first was not approved. He
was paid for the completed version
on August 31 of the same year.
The inscription was composed by

Bartolomeo di ser Benedetto Fortini
and read: IOHANNES ACUTUS EQUES
BRITANNICUS DUX AETATIS SUAE
CAUTISSIMUS ET REI MILITARIS
PERITISSIMUS HABITUS EST. Beneath is
the signature: PAULI UCCELLI OPUS.
The fresco was restored in 1524 by
Lorenzo di Credi (Longhi believes
Uccello retouched it when Andrea
del Castagno was executing his
similar equestrian portrait of Niccolò
da Tolentino about 1456), and
restored again, according to Baldinucci, about 1688. The decorative
border with griffins and candelabra
was added in the sixteenth century.
In 1842 it was transferred to canvas
and hung on the west wall of the
church, over the left entrance. In
1947 it was returned to its original
site. The work has been mentioned
in numerous records and Vasari
states that it would have been a
perfect work if Uccello had not
represented the horse "as moving
his legs on one side only, a thing
horses cannot do without falling."
Baldinucci and Cicognara demon-
strated that this fault does not in
fact exist. (See also plates 11 and 116.)

Plate 11

SIR JOHN HAWKWOOD. Detail:
rider and horse.

Plate 12

STORIES OF THE HOLY FATHERS.
*Frescoes, large lunette about 240 × 340;
sections within the fascias about 130–140
× 270–480. Florence, Convent of San
Miniato al Monte (gallery above the cloister).* Mentioned by Albertini ("in the
first cloister, above it, are XII paintings by Paolo Uccello," 1510), in the
Libro di Antonio Billi, in the *Anonimo
Gaddiano*, and by Vasari as follows:
"In San Miniato, outside Florence,
he did the cloister partly in *verde
terra* and partly in color, representing
the lives of the Holy Fathers. But he

50

did not observe a proper consistency in the use of his colors, for he made his fields blue, his city red, and his buildings of various hues according to his fancy. In this he was at fault, for buildings which are represented to be of stone cannot and ought not to be colored another tint." During the seventeenth and eighteenth centuries the frescoes were covered by plaster and partly destroyed. In 1925, some fragments were discovered by Marangoni, and he published the more important ones ("Gli affreschi di Paolo Uccello a San Miniato al Monte," in *Rivista d'Arte*, XII, 1930, pp. 403–17). Marangoni dates them before *The Flood* (see plate 44). Other fragments, which came to light in 1942, were published by Salmi ("Riflessioni su Paolo Uccello," in *Commentari*, I, 1950, pp. 23–26). The numerous sunken panels and general serious condition make identification of the scenes very difficult. Some of these represent St Benedict. The frescoes are on two parallel wings of the gallery. What was salvaged was published by Baldaccini in Salmi's essay. Their attribution to Uccello has been accepted with the exception of Berenson who assigned them to Giovanni di Francesco del Cervelliera, the so-called Carrand Master. Among suggested dates (about 1440 by Marangoni, Pudelko, Pittaluga, etc., and about 1425 by Boeck), that proposed by Salmi, shortly before 1439, seems the most likely. He recognized the hand of an assistant in the frescoes on the south wing. This plate reproduces the seventh scene in the east wing: probably a story from the life of St Benedict. (See also plates 13–20.)

Plate 13
STORIES OF THE HOLY FATHERS. First scene in the east wing.

Plate 14
STORIES OF THE HOLY FATHERS. Detail: plate 12: St Benedict (?)

Plate 15
STORIES OF THE HOLY FATHERS. Figure of a monk in the fifth scene in the east wing.

Plate 16
STORIES OF THE HOLY FATHERS. Figure of a praying monk in the fourth scene in the east wing.

Plate 17
STORIES OF THE HOLY FATHERS. Figure of angel in the fourth scene in the east wing.

Plate 18
STORIES OF THE HOLY FATHERS. Detail: plate 16.

Plate 19
STORIES OF THE HOLY FATHERS. Detail: plate 17.

Plate 20
STORIES OF THE HOLY FATHERS. Figure in the first scene in the south wing.

Plate 21
ST GEORGE AND THE DRAGON. *Panel, 52 × 90. Paris, Musée Jacquemart-André.* Acquired from the sale of the Bardini Collection, Florence (London, 1899). It was first attributed to Uccello by Loeser (1898), and this attribution is accepted, with the exception of Horne, Adolfo Venturi and Schubring, who think it is a product of Uccello's workshop or school. Pudelko considers it by the Master of the Karlsruhe "Adoration." It has been dated over different periods of Uccello's activity. The most probable date is the one proposed by Salmi, close to the *Stories of the Holy Fathers* in San

Miniato (around 1437–40). As Salmi observes, the different opinions are due, perhaps, to the bad condition of the panel (see also plate 22).

Plate 22

ST GEORGE AND THE DRAGON. Detail: the rescued princess.

Plate 23

PORTRAIT OF A LADY. *Panel, 39 × 26. New York, Metropolitan Museum of Art (Bache Collection).* Previously in the Holford Collection, London. Fischel believes it represents Elisabetta di Montefeltro, wife of Roberto Malatesta. It has been subject to various attributions. At one time it was thought to be Umbrian-Florentine and was assigned to Domenico Veneziano (Berenson, Mayer, etc.) and also the Master of the Castello "Nativity" (Offner, Lipman, Pope-Hennessy), and to the Master of the Karlsruhe "Adoration" (Pudelko). Leonello Venturi (1930) was the first to attribute it to Uccello, and later Salmi and Pittaluga agreed with him. I confirm this attribution and date it near the Prato frescoes, reproduced in the following plates.

Plate 24

THE BIRTH OF THE VIRGIN. *Fresco, 280 × 290. Prato, Cathedral, Capella dell'Assunta.* The Capella dell'Assunta, to the right of the Capella Maggiore in the Cathedral in Prato (at one time wrongly called the Capella Bocchineri) was founded in 1418 and its fresco decorations were executed by several Florentine artists during the first half of the fifteenth century. Among them Sirèn (1904) identified Andrea di Giusto as having painted the following scenes: *The Marriage of the Virgin, The Stoning of St Stephen,* and *The Finding of the Body of St Stephen.* These identifications are unanimously accepted. Various attributions have been made for the remaining scenes: *The Birth of the Virgin* (reproduced in this plate), *The Presentation of the Virgin in the Temple* (plate 25) and *The Dispute of St Stephen* (plate 26), the figures of saints on the large arch over the entrance to the Chapel: *St Dominic, St Jerome* (both in plate 30), *St Paul, St Francis* (both in plate 31), *Blessed Jacopone da Todi* (plate 29; detached and removed to the Sacristy), the *Four Cardinal Virtues* on the roof of the Chapel, and also the *clypei* circling the heads (plate 32). They have been assigned to Domenico Veneziano (Schmarsow); to Giovanni di Francesco del Cervelliera, the so-called Carrand Master (Longhi in 1928 and Berenson); to an unknown pupil of Uccello identified by some critics as the Master of the Karlsruhe "Adoration," or as the Master of the Quarata Predella (see plates 40–41); Pope-Hennessy calls him the Prato Master. The attribution to Uccello was initiated by Longhi (1940) and Ragghianti. The latter observed that 1445 being generally considered as a *terminus post quem* for the completion of the frescoes has no bearing on them, and he is therefore inclined to date them before 1445. This is my opinion too, and excluding Uccello's direct participation in weaker parts (like the *Virtues* on the roof), the other frescoes were executed by Uccello soon after 1436. Despite his conclusions being different, I should like to draw the reader's attention to Mario Salmi's excellent study: "Paolo Uccello, Domenico Veneziano, Piero della Francesca e gli affreschi del Duomo di Prato," in *Bollettino d'Arte del Ministero della Educazione Nazionale, XXVIII,* 1934, 1, pp. 1–27. (See detail on plate 28 and plates 25–32.)

Plate 25

THE PRESENTATION OF THE VIRGIN IN THE TEMPLE. *Fresco, 280 × 340. Prato, Cathedral, Capella dell'Assunta*. See general comment on plate 24.

Plate 26

THE DISPUTE OF ST STEPHEN. *Fresco, 280 × 290. Prato, Cathedral, Capella dell'Assunta*. See comment on plate 24 and detail in plate 27.

Plate 27

THE DISPUTE OF ST STEPHEN. Detail: spectators.

Plate 28

THE BIRTH OF THE VIRGIN. Detail: figures of women.

Plate 29

BLESSED JACOPONE DA TODI. *Fresco transferred to canvas, 120 × 60. Prato, Cathedral, Sacristy (detached from the Capella dell'Assunta)*. See comment on plate 24.

Plate 30

ST DOMINIC and ST JEROME. *Frescoes, 120 × 46. Prato, Cathedral, Capella dell'Assunta*. See comment on plate 24.

Plate 31

ST PAUL and ST FRANCIS. *Frescoes, 120 × 46. Prato, Cathedral, Capella dell'Assunta*. See commentary on plate 24.

Plate 32

CLYPEI WITH HEADS. *Frescoes, diameter of each 26. Prato, Cathedral, Capella dell'Assunta*. See comment on plate 24.

Plate 33

ST MONICA WITH TWO CHILDREN. *Fragment (79 × 35) of right section of panel. Florence, Contini-Bonacossi Collection. At left are traces of the figure at the center*. Published by Longhi (1928) as a work by Giovanni di Francesco del Cervelliera, and identified as St Scholastica. Having later ascribed the Prato frescoes to Uccello (see comment on plate 24), Longhi also attributed this panel to Uccello. Salmi and Pudelko believe it to be by Uccello, Oertel and Boeck attribute it to the Master of the "Scenes from the Life of St Benedict" in the upper cloister of the Badia, Florence. I confirm the ascription to Uccello, and date the work about 1440.

Plate 34

FOUR HEADS OF PROPHETS. *Frescoes, diameter of each 68. Florence, Duomo*. In four apertures at the corners of the clock-face. In 1933, Poggi published two records of payments to Uccello for the decoration of the clock-face in Santa Maria del Fiore (the Duomo), dated respectively February 22 and April 2, 1443. They were therefore executed in 1443 (but Ragghianti dates them 1437). They are recorded by Vasari: "At the same time [as *Sir John Hawkwood*] and in the same church, he executed the clock-face in color, over the principal door inside the church, together with four heads done in fresco in the corners." The fresco is well preserved, with the exception of the head in the bottom left corner. (This plate reproduces the first of the four heads. See also plates 35–37.)

Plate 35

HEAD OF PROPHET. See comment on plate 34.

Plate 36

HEAD OF PROPHET. See comment on plate 34.

Plate 37

HEAD OF PROPHET. See comment on plate 34.

Plate 38

THE NATIVITY and THE RESURRECTION. *Circular windows, diameters respectively 473 and 468. Florence, Duomo.* Ghiberti, Donatello, Andrea del Castagno and Uccello supplied the cartoons for the eight large circular stained-glass windows in the cupola of Santa Maria del Fiore. Uccello was paid on May 2, 1443 for an *Ascension*, but a cartoon supplied by Ghiberti was chosen for the execution of this scene. On July 8, 1443, Uccello was paid for the cartoon of *The Resurrection* which was executed on glass by the glass-painter, Bernardo di Francesco. On November 5, 1443, the artist was paid for *The Nativity* which was executed on glass by Angiolo di Lippo. Finally, on February 8, 1444, he was paid for an *Annunciation* which was executed by Bernardo di Francesco and was destroyed in 1828. A document dated January 28, 1445 seems to deal with Uccello's repairs to the cartoons rather than with the restoration of the windows, as Van Straelen has suggested. Later restorations are to be seen particularly in the body of Christ in *The Resurrection*.

Plate 39

VIRGIN AND CHILD. *Panel, 57 × 33. Dublin, National Gallery of Ireland.* Acquired from the Bardini sale in London, 1899, where the work was attributed to Lorentino d'Andrea. The attribution to Uccello was first proposed by Pudelko (1936), followed by Salmi and Ragghianti. Pope-Hennessy believes it to be by the Prato Master. I confirm the attribution to Uccello and date it shortly before 1450.

Plates 40–41

THE ADORATION OF THE MAGI. *Together with* ST JOHN ON PATMOS (*plate 42*) *and* TWO KNEELING SAINTS (*plate 43*), *the works form a panel, 21 × 178. Bagno a Ripoli, Florence, Church of San Bartolommeo a Quarata.* The three paintings constitute a predella of a lost altarpiece. They were published for the first time by Marangoni (1931–32) as one of Uccello's early works. The attribution has been accepted by Serra, Ragghianti, Boeck and by Longhi who believes it to have been painted around 1445–50. Gamba believes them to be by a follower of Uccello; Berenson, by Giovanni di Francesco del Cervelliera; Pudelko, by the Master of the Karlsruhe "Adoration." Salmi and Pope-Hennessy link them with the Prato frescoes (plate 24)—Salmi as by the Master of the Quarata Predella, and Pope-Hennessy as by the Prato Master. I confirm the attribution to Uccello and date them shortly after 1440. (See plates 42–43.)

Plate 42

ST JOHN ON PATMOS. Left panel of the Quarata Predella. See comment on plates 40–41.

Plate 43

TWO KNEELING SAINTS. Right panel of the Quarata Predella. See comment on plates 40–41.

Plate 44

THE FLOOD AND THE RECESSION OF THE FLOOD. *Fresco, 215 × 510. Florence, Convent of Santa Maria Novella, Chiostro Verde (under the first arch, extension of the east wing).* This, together with *The Sacrifice of Noah and the Drunkenness of Noah* which are frescoed below (see plates 53–59) is mentioned by Manetti and by earliest records. They are described in detail by Vasari who above all admired *The Flood* as being the greatest expression of Uccello's art: "... he painted the Flood and Noah's ark, representing the dead, the tempest, the fury of the winds, the flashes of lightning, the rooting up of trees, and the terror of men, with such pains and with so much art and diligence, that no more can be said. In perspective, he has represented a dead body, foreshortened, the eyes of which are being pecked out by a crow, and a drowned child, whose body, being full of water, is bloated. He further represented various human emotions, such as the disregard of the water by two fighting men on horseback, the extreme terror of death of a woman and a man who are riding astride a buffalo; but in sinking, they are despairing of all hope of safety. The work is of such quality and excellence that Paolo acquired the greatest fame from it. . . . He also painted the drunkenness of Noah, with his contemptuous son, Ham, in whom he portrayed his friend Dello, a Florentine painter and sculptor, together with his other sons, Shem and Japhet, who cover the shameful naked body of their father. He painted a cask in perspective, with lines curving in different directions, which is considered very fine. . . . He further made the sacrifice of Noah, the ark being open in perspective, with ranges of perches in the upper parts divided into regular rows where the birds are stationed, which fly out in flocks foreshortened in several directions. In the air appears God the Father above the sacrifice which Noah and his sons are making. This is the most difficult figure represented by Paolo in all his works, because it is flying toward the wall with the head foreshortened, and it has such force, and is in such strong relief, that it has the appearance of forcing its way through. . . . In short, this work has so much harmony and grace that it is beyond comparison the best of all his works, and has been greatly praised not only in those times but also now." The upper and lower frescoes were detached from the wall by D. Fiscali in 1909, and certain differences between the cartoon underneath *The Drunkenness of Noah* and the fresco came to light. *The Flood* is fairly well preserved with only a few sunken parts; the two scenes below (*The Sacrifice and The Drunkenness*) are ruined and some parts have been obliterated. Using ancient engravings, like *The Sacrifice of Noah* engraved for Seroux d'Agincourt (*Histoire de l'Art par les Monuments*, 1823), and *The Drunkenness of Noah* by Calendi (*L'Etruria Pittrice*, 1791), it is possible to reconstruct the frescoes. But the latter engraving seems partly incorrect. With the exception of Berenson who considers these frescoes as executed by Uccello at an early age, the frescoes are unanimously believed to be either of a much later date than the stories from Genesis under the first extension of the wing (see plates 1–9), or else completely renewed by Uccello following rapid deterioration of the first frescoes. Considering that Dello Delli (who, according to Vasari, seems to be portrayed in Ham) had returned to Florence from Spain in 1446–48, the frescoes are generally dated in these years. Longhi has proposed a date between 1455 and 1460. Accepting Pope-Hennessy's theory that the perspective and composition of *The Flood* were influenced by Donatello's bronze reliefs on the altar of the Church of Sant'Antonio in Padua, I agree that these frescoes should be dated around 1450. (See plates 45–52 and 53–59.)

Plate 45

THE FLOOD AND THE RECESSION OF THE FLOOD. Detail: swimming figures.

Plate 46

THE FLOOD AND THE RECESSION OF THE FLOOD. Detail: Noah in prayer.

Plate 47

THE FLOOD AND THE RECESSION OF THE FLOOD. Detail: Noah's head.

Plate 48

THE FLOOD AND THE RECESSION OF THE FLOOD. Detail: Noah and God the Father.

Color Plate I

THE FLOOD. Detail of plate 44.

Plate 49

THE FLOOD AND THE RECESSION OF THE FLOOD. Detail: male figure.

Plate 50

THE FLOOD AND THE RECESSION OF THE FLOOD. Detail: male figure.

Plate 51

THE FLOOD AND THE RECESSION OF THE FLOOD. Detail: male figure.

Plate 52

THE FLOOD AND THE RECESSION OF THE FLOOD. Detail: a man's head.

Plate 53

THE SACRIFICE OF NOAH AND THE DRUNKENNESS OF NOAH. *Fresco, 277 × 540. Florence, Convent of Santa Maria Novella, Chiostro Verde (under the fourth arch, extension of the east wing).* See comment on plate 44 and plates 54–59.

Plate 54

THE SACRIFICE OF NOAH AND THE DRUNKENNESS OF NOAH. Detail: God the Father.

Plate 55

THE SACRIFICE OF NOAH AND THE DRUNKENNESS OF NOAH. Detail: heads of figures taking part in the sacrifice.

Plate 56

THE SACRIFICE OF NOAH AND THE DRUNKENNESS OF NOAH. Detail: Ham and Shem.

Plate 57

THE SACRIFICE OF NOAH AND THE DRUNKENNESS OF NOAH. Detail: Shem and Japhet.

Plate 58

THE SACRIFICE OF NOAH AND THE DRUNKENNESS OF NOAH. Detail: head of Ham.

Plate 59

THE SACRIFICE OF NOAH AND THE DRUNKENNESS OF NOAH. Detail: head of Shem.

Plate 60

THE DEAD CHRIST BETWEEN THE VIRGIN AND ST JOHN THE EVANGELIST. *Panel, 22 × 177. Avane, Florence, Oratory of the Church of the Annunziata.* Bears the date 1452. It was attributed to Uccello by Longhi (1940). Pope-Hennessy assigns the panel to the Prato Master.

Plate 61

THE NATIVITY AND THE ANNUNCIATION TO THE SHEPHERDS. *Detached fresco, 140 × 215. Florence, Cloister of the ex-Hospital of San Martino alla Scala.* It was first published as Uccello's work by Paatz in 1934 ("Una 'Natività' di Paolo

Uccello e alcune considerazioni sull'arte del Maestro," in *Rivista d'Arte*, XVI, 1934, pp. 111–48) who dated it around 1446. This date was accepted by Boeck and by Salmi, but the latter believes it a product of Uccello's workshop. Pope-Hennessy is inclined to date it in the sixth rather than in the fifth decade of the century. The fresco is in a poor condition and in part undecipherable, and it is therefore not possible to establish whether an assistant or a pupil has helped in the execution. The idea for the composition was certainly Uccello's.

Plate 62
THE FOUNDERS OF FLORENTINE ART. *Panel, 42 × 210. Paris, Louvre.* It was acquired in 1847 at the Stevens sale, and was in such a bad state and so repainted that it seemed to justify the great differences of opinion. Moreover, Vasari describes a panel representing the five people portrayed here—Giotto, Uccello, Donatello, Antonio Manetti and Filippo Brunelleschi (whose identity is doubtful because an inscription giving the names has been repainted)—in the first edition of his *Lives* (1550) as a work by Masaccio hanging in the house of Giuliano di Sangallo. But in the second edition (1568), he attributes it to Uccello. Some critics have thought it was painted by Masaccio or by his school (Beenken, Lanyi, Longhi); others consider it a late-sixteenth-century copy (Cavalcaselle, Benkard, Ragghianti); the majority link it in more or less directly with Uccello (Berenson, Horne, Lipman, Boeck, Van Marle, Schubring, Pudelko, Salmi, Pittaluga, Pope-Hennessy, etc.). Despite recent restorations and the removal of rough repaintings it is still difficult to give a definite opinion. But one

should probably link it with Uccello. The date frequently suggested is between 1450 and 1460. (See also plates 63–65.)

Plate 63
THE FOUNDERS OF FLORENTINE ART. Detail: Donatello and Filippo Brunelleschi.

Plate 64
THE FOUNDERS OF FLORENTINE ART. Detail: Giotto.

Color Plate II
THE SACRIFICE OF NOAH AND THE DRUNKENNESS OF NOAH. Detail of plate 53.

Plate 65
THE FOUNDERS OF FLORENTINE ART. Detail: Paolo Uccello.

Plate 66
ST GEORGE AND THE DRAGON. *Canvas, 57 × 73. London, National Gallery (formerly Vienna, Lanckoronski Collection).* It was first attributed to Uccello by Loeser (1898). The attribution is generally accepted, with exception of Adolfo Venturi (to "an excellent painter of *cassoni*"), Berenson (to Giovanni di Francesco del Cervelliera) and Pudelko (to the Master of the Karlsruhe "Adoration"). Among different dates suggested, the most probable is around 1456—if, as Boeck has observed, an echo of the horse in the portrait of Niccolò da Tolentino by Andrea del Castagno can be seen in St George's horse. (See also plate 67.)

Plate 67
ST GEORGE AND THE DRAGON. Detail: horse and rider.

Plates 68–69
THE BATTLE OF SAN ROMANO. *Panel, 182 × 317. London, National*

Gallery. The earliest record of this and the other two panels of the same subject (now in the Uffizi, plates 80–91 and in the Louvre, plates 92–99) was published by Horne in 1901; it is an inventory of the contents of the Palazzo Medici drawn up in 1492. According to this, in the "large room on the ground floor, called the Chamera di Lorenzo" there are "six paintings in a gold frame, 42 *braccia* long and 3½ *braccia* [arm-lengths] high, and placed against cypress backing and above the couch. There are three of the rout of San Romano; one of a combat between dragons and lions, and one of a scene from the legend of Paris, [all five] by the hand of Pagolo Uccello; and one representing a chase by Francesco di Pesello." The *Codice Magliabechiano*, the *Anonimo Gaddiano*, and Vasari describe them as "paintings of *giostre* [tournaments]" or "displays [evidently for tournaments] of armed men on horseback, of those times." According to an inventory of 1598 they were removed from their original place, as it describes them as "three large ancient paintings of *giostre* all in one piece, with small frames in gold, placed high above the floor of the first chamber at the entrance to the chapel." Before Horne's publication of the 1492 inventory, the three panels were identified with the four battles which Vasari notes were painted by Uccello for the Casa de' Bartolini at Valfonda. But these were monochromes and had been repainted by Giuliano Bugiardini. The panels in London and Paris were purchased by the Lombardi-Baldi Collection from the Giraldi family between 1844 and 1848. The first of these was purchased with the Lombardi-Baldi Collection by the National Gallery in 1857, and the second was purchased from the Campana Collection by the Musée Napoleon III. The Uffizi panel has been in the gallery since 1769. The three panels are in different states, because of varying degrees of restoration (the London panel is slightly blurred due to over-cleaning prior to its acquisition and the other two are better preserved even if old varnish has oxidized). The panels have been differently dated. They are considered Uccello's early work by Cavalcaselle, Marangoni and Antal. Pudelko believed them painted around 1445, and other critics suggest a date between 1445 and 1460. Salmi has linked them with the equestrian monument to Niccolò da Tolentino, commissioned from Andrea del Castagno in 1456. Pope-Hennessy believes them to have been commissioned by Cosimo de Medici in 1456. One may therefore assume that they were completed between 1456 and 1460. (See plates 70–79, 80–91, and 92–99.)

Plate 70
THE BATTLE OF SAN ROMANO. *London*. Detail: Niccolò da Tolentino on horseback.

Plate 71
THE BATTLE OF SAN ROMANO. *London*. Detail: knights duelling.

Plate 72
THE BATTLE OF SAN ROMANO. *London*. Detail: head of a page.

Plate 73
THE BATTLE OF SAN ROMANO. *London*. Detail: head of Niccolò da Tolentino.

Plate 74
THE BATTLE OF SAN ROMANO. *London*. Detail: heads of trumpeters.

Plate 75
THE BATTLE OF SAN ROMANO. *London*. Detail: knights in plate 71.

Plate 76

THE BATTLE OF SAN ROMANO. *London*. Detail: pieces of armor, poles, and a helmet scattered over the ground.

Plate 77

THE BATTLE OF SAN ROMANO. *London*. Detail: body of a warrior.

Plate 78

THE BATTLE OF SAN ROMANO. *London*. Detail: knights on foot in the background.

Plate 79

THE BATTLE OF SAN ROMANO. *London*. Detail: emblem of Niccolò da Tolentino.

Plates 80–81

THE BATTLE OF SAN ROMANO. *Panel, 182 × 323. Florence, Uffizi.* See comment on plates 68–69, and plates 82–91.

Plate 82

THE BATTLE OF SAN ROMANO. *Florence*. Detail: Bernardino della Ciarda being unhorsed.

Plate 83

THE BATTLE OF SAN ROMANO. *Florence*. Detail: Sienese knights.

Plate 84

THE BATTLE OF SAN ROMANO. *Florence*. Detail: plate 82.

Plate 85

THE BATTLE OF SAN ROMANO. *Florence*. Detail: heads of knights on foot and horses.

Plate 86

THE BATTLE OF SAN ROMANO. *Florence*. Detail: Florentine foot-soldiers and bowmen.

Plate 87

THE BATTLE OF SAN ROMANO. *Florence*. Detail: heads of foot-soldiers.

Plate 88

THE BATTLE OF SAN ROMANO. *Florence*. Detail: Sienese knights.

Color Plate III

THE BATTLE OF SAN ROMANO. Detail of plates 80–81.

Plate 89

THE BATTLE OF SAN ROMANO. *Florence*. Detail: trumpeter.

Plate 90

THE BATTLE OF SAN ROMANO. *Florence*. Detail: warrior in the background.

Plate 91

THE BATTLE OF SAN ROMANO. *Florence*. Detail: warrior in the background.

Plates 92–93

THE BATTLE OF SAN ROMANO. *Panel, 180 × 316. Paris, Louvre.* See comment on plates 68–69 and plates 94–99.

Plate 94

THE BATTLE OF SAN ROMANO. *Paris*. Detail: attacking knights.

Plate 95

THE BATTLE OF SAN ROMANO. *Paris*. Detail: heads of knights and horses.

Plate 96

THE BATTLE OF SAN ROMANO. *Paris*. Detail: waiting knights.

Color Plate IV

THE PROFANATION OF THE HOST. Detail of plate 106.

Plate 97

THE BATTLE OF SAN ROMANO. *Paris*. Detail: head of foot-soldier.

Plate 98

THE BATTLE OF SAN ROMANO. *Paris*. Detail: Micheletto Attendolo da Cotignola.

Plate 99

THE BATTLE OF SAN ROMANO. *Paris*. Detail: head of Micheletto Attendolo da Cotignola.

Plates 100–101

HUNT BY NIGHT. *Panel, 65 × 165. Oxford, Ashmolean Museum*. This panel was in the Fox-Strongways Collection from 1850. It was most probably the front of a *cassone* and was first attributed to Uccello by Loeser (1898). The attribution has been accepted, with the exception of Adolfo Venturi and Schlosser. Marangoni and Van Marle think it an early work by Uccello, before 1436. But all other critics agree that it must be a later work, after 1460. The panel is well preserved. (See also plates 102–105.)

Plate 102

HUNT BY NIGHT. Detail: left side of panel.

Plate 103

HUNT BY NIGHT. Detail: center of panel.

Plate 104

HUNT BY NIGHT. Detail: center.

Plate 105

HUNT BY NIGHT. Detail: figure of hunter at right of panel.

Plates 106–108

THE PROFANATION OF THE HOST. *Predella, 42 × 351. Urbino, Galleria Nazionale delle Marche*. This predella was transferred to the Ducal Palace in 1861 from the Collegio degli Scopoli, adjacent to the Church of Sant'Agata which had inherited the contents of the demolished Church of Corpus Domini. There, the panel was on the high altar, serving as a predella for *The Institution of the Eucharist* painted in 1473 by the Flemish artist, Justus of Ghent (it had originally been planned as a predella for a painting which Piero della Francesca declined to execute). Documents as far back as 1465 state the presence of Uccello in Urbino and his connections with the Company of Corpus Domini. From February 6, 1467 until October 17, 1469, a series of payments to Uccello for the predella are recorded. Some of the payments took the form of a jacket, stockings, shoes and cloth. The panel is fairly well preserved. The source of the legend illustrated in the predella is obscure. The legend is represented in six scenes: (i) a woman offers a Host to a pawnbroker to obtain the return of her coat; (ii) the broker places the Host on a fire from which blood miraculously streams, while outside armed men try to force open the door to arrest the sacrilegious couple; (iii) a solemn procession returns the Host to the church where it will be placed on the altar; (iv) the woman is executed and an angel intervenes to promise salvation for her repentance; (v) armed men and soldiers burn the broker and his family; (vi) angels and devils fight for possession of the woman's soul —her corpse lies before the altar. (See also plates 109–113.)

Plate 109

THE PROFANATION OF THE HOST. Detail of second scene: the broker's wife and children stand terrified before the blood flowing from the Host.

Plate 110

THE PROFANATION OF THE HOST. Detail of second scene: armed men trying to break down the door of the broker's house.

Plate 111

THE PROFANATION OF THE HOST. Detail of fourth scene: knights present at the hanging of the woman.

Plate 112

THE PROFANATION OF THE HOST.
Detail of fourth scene: the woman
about to be hanged.

Plate 113

THE PROFANATION OF THE HOST.
Detail of fifth scene: the burning
pawnbroker and his family.

Plate 114

CHRIST ON THE CROSS WITH
THE VIRGIN AND SS JOHN THE
BAPTIST, JOHN THE EVANGELIST
AND FRANCIS. *Panel, 46 × 67.
Lugano (Castagnola), Thyssen Collection.*
Attributed to Uccello by Van Marle
(1928), followed by Marangoni,
Lionello Venturi, Salmi, Boeck and
Pittaluga. Berenson believes it was
executed by Giovanni di Francesco
del Cervelliera. Pudelko and Pope-
Hennessy attributes it to the Master
of the Karlsruhe "Adoration." I
reconfirm the attribution to Uccello
and date the panel rather later, close
to *The Profanation of the Host.* The
crucifix has been slightly restored.
(See also plate 115.)

Plate 115

CHRIST ON THE CROSS WITH
THE VIRGIN AND SS JOHN THE
BAPTIST, JOHN THE EVANGELIST
AND FRANCIS. Detail: SS John the
Evangelist and Francis.

Plate 116

DRAWING FOR SIR JOHN HAWK-
WOOD. *Silverpoint heightened in white
on a prepared light green ground, with a
background in dull red; squared for
enlargement; 46 × 33. Florence, Uffizi
(Gabinetto dei Disegni).* Unanimously
attributed to Uccello, this is considered a precious preparatory study
for the fresco in Santa Maria del
Fiore (plate 10). Marangoni has
rightly pointed out that the drawing
has greater stylistic discipline than
the fresco, and the geometrical

character of the fresco may have
been affected by restorations carried
out about 1688.

Plate 117

HEAD OF A MAN IN PROFILE.
*Bister wash on white paper, 29 × 20.5.
Florence, Uffizi (Gabinetto dei Disegni).*
Attributed to Uccello by Berenson.
The attribution was accepted by
Salmi, Boeck, Pope-Hennessy and
others. Beenken suggests Masaccio,
while Stix and Frohlich-Bum are
doubtful. I reconfirm the attribution
to Uccello.

Plate 118

A MOUNTED KNIGHT. *Pen and
silverpoint heightened in white on
greenish prepared paper; squared; 30 ×
34. Florence, Uffizi (Gabinetto dei
Disegni).* Unanimously attributed to
Uccello. Some critics thought the
drawing a *St George*, others a study
for one of the knights in the Uffizi
panel of *The Battle of San Romano*
(plates 80–81). Berenson believed it
a preparatory study for one of the
four battle scenes recorded by Vasari
in the Casa Bartolini, and later lost.
(See comment on plates 68–69.)

Plate 119

PERSPECTIVE STUDY OF A
CHALICE. *Pen on white paper, 29 ×
24.5. Florence, Uffizi (Gabinetto dei
Disegni).* This and the two perspective studies of *mazzocchi* (male head-
dress common in Florence, second
half of the fifteenth century, see plate
120), are examples of exercises in
perspective which occupied Uccello
especially, as Vasari relates, towards
the end of his life. Their attribution
to Uccello is unanimously accepted.

Plate 120

PERSPECTIVE STUDIES OF TWO
"MAZZOCCHI." *Pen on white paper,
respectively 9 × 27 and 9 × 24.
Florence, Uffizi (Gabinetto dei Disegni).*
See comment on plate 119.

LOST PAINTINGS

SS COSMAS AND DAMIAN. *Florence, Church of the Carmine, Capella di San Gerolamo*. Recorded by Vasari ("reredos of St Cosmas and St Damian") and also by Baldinucci. Salmi tentatively suggests that the remains of this work, which would have been an early painting, might be identified with the *St Cosmas* and *St Damian* in the Staatliches Museen, Berlin (Nos. 1141 C and D).

ST PETER. *Venice, Basilica of St Mark, façade*. Mosaic, 1425. The work is recorded in a letter sent from the Office of Works of Santa Maria del Fiore to Pietro Beccanugi, Florentine Ambassador in Venice, on March 23, 1432. The letter asked for information about Uccello's ability to execute mosaics. Salmi pointed out and illustrated that there is a reminder of the figure of the Saint in *The Procession of the Relic of the Cross in St Mark's Square* by Gentile Bellini (Accademia, Venice). (See "Riflessioni su Paolo Uccello," in *Commentari*, I, 1950, pp. 22–23.)

TWO FIGURES. *Florence, Convent of Annalena*. Probably frescoes on the façade of the Convent. Ascribed to Uccello in the *Codice Magliabechiano*, the *Libro di Antonio Billi*, and by Vasari.

ST ANTHONY THE ABBOT BETWEEN SS COSMAS AND DAMIAN. *Florence, Hospital of Lelmo (now the Accademia)*. Fresco. Mentioned by Vasari as among Uccello's "first pictures," and situated "in an oblong niche painted in perspective."

SCENES FROM THE LIFE OF ST FRANCIS. *Florence, Church of Santa Trinità*. Frescoes on the entrance wall of the Church. Manetti mentions them rather vaguely ("many . . . things"). Albertini specifies them as being "between the doors of the façade." Vasari gives a fuller description of the scenes: "he painted stories of St Francis in fresco— namely, the receiving of the Stigmata; the supporting of the Church, which he holds up with his shoulders; and his meeting with St Dominic." Vasari records that the frescoes were "inside the Church, over the left-hand door." Baldinucci says that they were "over the door in the center." Pudelko identifies a damaged seraph as being part of the scene representing *St Francis Receiving the Stigmata*.

THE ANNUNCIATION. *Florence, Church of Santa Maria Maggiore*. Fresco. Mentioned by Albertini and described thus by Vasari: "he worked also in Santa Maria Maggiore, in a chapel near the side door which leads to San Giovanni, where there are the panel and predella by Masaccio. Here he executed an Annunciation in fresco, in which he made a building worthy of consideration. This was something new and difficult in those times, seeing that it was the first possessing any beauty of manner. This was seen by craftsmen and showed them how to manage the receding of lines with grace and proportion, and how to extend a level space which is small and confined so that it appears far distant and large. And when men with judgment and grace can add to this shadows and light by means of colors in their proper places, there is no doubt that they cause an illusion to the eye, so that the painting seems to be real and in relief. And not being satisfied with this, he wished to demonstrate even greater difficulties in some columns, which, foreshortened in perspective, curve round and break the salient angle of the vaulting in which the four Evangelists are represented; this thing was held something beautiful and difficult, and, in truth, in that branch of his profession Paolo was ingenious and able." Salmi and Pudelko think that the scheme of Uccello's lost fresco is reflected in an *Annunciation* attributed to Paolo Schiavo in the Collegiata at Castiglione d'Olona.

THE ANNUNCIATION. *Florence, Duomo.* Large stained-glass window for the drum under the cupola. A documented work, which was executed after a drawing by Uccello, by Bernardo di Francesco in 1444. It was destroyed in 1828.

PAINTING OF A TABERNACLE. *Florence, Church of San Giovanni.* A document of payment exists for this work.

THE BLESSED ANDREA CORSINI. *Florence, Duomo, Library.* Fresco. According to Milanesi, this was executed in 1453.

DRAWINGS FOR TWO LARGE STAINED-GLASS WINDOWS. *Florence, Duomo.* Executed in collaboration with the master glazier, Bernardo di Francesco. A documented work.

SCENES FROM THE LEGEND OF PARIS. *Florence, Palazzo Medici.* Tempera on canvas. Besides the three *Battle of San Romano* panels, the 1492 inventory of the Palazzo Medici records that also in Lorenzo's chamber was a picture of "battles between dragons and lions, and one with the Legend of Paris by Pagolo Uccello." Vasari writes: "in the same house, among other pictures of animals, he made some lions, which were fighting one another with such fierceness and movement, that they seemed to be alive. But the rarest scene of all was one in which a serpent, fighting a lion, showed its ferocity by violent movements, while poison spurted out of its mouth and eyes; at the same time a country girl who is present, is looking after an ox made with the most beautiful foreshortening. The actual drawing for this ox, by the hand of Paolo, is in my books of drawings, and also that of the peasant girl, full of fear, and in the act of running away from the animals. There are likewise certain very lifelike shepherds, and a landscape which was considered something very beautiful in his time." The fight between the serpent (a dragon) and the lion is recorded in the 1598 inventory. The identity of the second painting, described by Vasari as the *Legend of Paris* and which is listed in the 1492 inventory, has not been established. Salmi has distinguished some motifs clearly based on these lost compositions in a series of prints dating from the second half of the fifteenth century.

SCENES FROM THE LIFE OF ST BENEDICT. *Florence, ex-Monastery* of the Angeli, *Chiostro dell'Orto*. The frescoes are mentioned in the *Codice Magliabechiano*, by the *Anonimo Gaddiano*, and in the *Libro di Antonio Billi*. Vasari writes: "he also wrought in *verde terra* the *loggia* that faces west above the garden of the Monastery of the Angeli, painting below each arch a story of St Benedict the Abbot, and of the most notable events of his life, up to his death. Here, among many beautiful scenes, is one in which a monastery is destroyed by the agency of the Devil, while a monk is left dead below the stones and beams. No less notable is the terror of another monk, whose draperies, as he flees, cling round his nude figure and flutter with the most beautiful grace; and by this, Paolo stirred the minds of craftsmen so much that they have followed his method ever since. Very beautiful, too, is the figure of St Benedict, in the scene in which, in the presence of his monks, he restores the dead monk to life with much dignity and devoutness. Finally, in all these stories there are features worthy of consideration, and above all in certain places where the very tiles on the roof, whether flat or round, are drawn in perspective. And in the death of St Benedict, while his monks are performing his obsequies and bewailing him, there are some sick men and cripples, all most beautiful, who stand gazing at him; and noteworthy, too, among the many loving and devout followers of the Saint, is an old monk with crutches under his arms, who has a marvelous expression on his face, revealing hopes of being made whole again. In this work there are no landscapes in color, nor many buildings, nor difficult perspectives, but there is truly great design, and much of it is very good indeed." Salmi suggests that a detail from

these frescoes may be reproduced in a drawing in the Uffizi (No. 97 E) by the School of Fra Angelico. It represents a monk teaching three other monks. Pope-Hennessy does not find this theory convincing.

FOUR BATTLE SCENES. *Florence, Casa Bartolini at Valfonda*. Panels. Vasari writes: "and in Gualfonda, in particular, on a terrace in the garden which once belonged to the Bartolini, there are four battle scenes that he painted on wood, full of horses and armed men, dressed in very beautiful costumes of those days; and among the men are portraits of Paolo Orsino, Ottobuono da Parma, Luca da Canale, and Carlo Malatesta, Lord of Rimini, all of whom were captains-general in those times. These pictures were spoiled and suffered injuries, and were restored in our own day by Giuliano Bugiardini, who did them more harm than good." Before the publication of the 1492 Medici inventory, these scenes were identified with the three panels of *The Battle of San Romano* (Horne, 1901). Horne believed that they were painted in *terra verde* in a *loggia* overlooking the Bartolini garden, and were destroyed in 1638.

GIANTS. *Padua, Casa Vitaliani*. Monochrome frescoes. They are recorded by the *Anonimo Morelliano*. Vasari writes: "Paolo was summoned to Padua by Donato [Donatello], when the latter was working there, and at the entrance of the house of the Vitali he painted some giants in *verde terra*, which, as I discovered in a Latin letter from Girolamo Campagnola to Messer Leonico Tomeo, the philosopher, are so beautiful that they were greatly admired by Andrea Mantegna." Fiocco's theory that some drawings in the *Chronicle* by Leonardo Besozzo

(Crespi-Morbio Collection, Milan) are adapted from these lost figures has been rejected by Salmi. He points out that the *Chronicle*, which dates from 1436 to 1442, was published before Uccello executed the frescoes (probably during the artist's second stay in Venice, in 1445). Readers are referred to Ragghianti's essay on these lost frescoes ("Casa Vitaliani, "in *La Critica d'Arte*, II, 1938, pp. 236 ff.).

CEILING REPRESENTING THE FOUR ELEMENTS. *Florence, Casa Peruzzi.* Fresco. Vasari writes: "Paolo wrought in fresco the ceiling in the house of the Peruzzi, with triangular sections in perspective, and in the angles of the corners he painted the four elements, making for each an appropriate animal: for the earth, a mole; for the water, a fish; for the fire, a salamander; and for the air, a chameleon, which lives on air and can assume any color. And because he had never seen a chameleon, he painted a camel with its mouth open, swallowing and filling its belly with air. Great, indeed, was his *naïveté* by using the name of the camel to allude to an animal that is like a little dry lizard, and representing it by a great uncouth beast."

CHRIST AND ST THOMAS. *Florence, Church of San Tommaso, above the entrance door.* Fresco (?). Mentioned in the *Codice Magliabechiano* and the *Libro di Antonio Billi*. Vasari refers to it as Uccello's "last work," and says that when Donatello saw it he criticized the old artist severely, with the words, "Ah, Paolo, now you ought to be closing shop, and instead here you are, opening!"

PAINTINGS ATTRIBUTED TO UCCELLO

Plate 121

PORTRAIT OF A YOUNG MAN. *Panel, 47 × 36. Chambéry, Musée Benoit-Molin.* On the parapet is the inscription: EL.FIN. FATVTTO. At one time believed a Venetian work, it was first attributed to Uccello by Longhi in 1927, followed by Pudelko, Lionello Venturi, Van Marle, Pope-Hennessy and, with reservations, Salmi. The attribution was rejected by Berenson (Masaccio?), Lipman (follower of Masaccio) and Boeck. Parts of the portrait seem repainted (Pudelko states that the hat has been repainted and that the inscription is a later addition—this last is improbable), and only a more careful direct study can lead to more accurate assessment. It is, anyway, very difficult to separate this work from the other two portraits of *Matteo Olivieri* and *Michele Olivieri* (plate 122) which are usually accepted as the work of Domenico Veneziano. If these are not by Veneziano, they are probably by his school.

Plate 122

PORTRAITS OF MATTEO OLIVIERI and MICHELE OLIVIERI. *Panels, 48 × 33 each. Respectively in Washington, D.C., National Gallery of Art (Mellon Collection) and New York, Rockefeller Collection.* Attributed to Uccello by Lionello Venturi, Boeck, Pudelko and Kennedy. More worthy of attention is the attribution to

Domenico Veneziano by Berenson and Salmi.

Plate 123

SCENES FROM MONASTIC LEGENDS. *Canvas, 81 × 110. Florence, Galleria dell' Accademia (from Santo Spirito alla Costa San Giorgio).* The work has been attributed directly to Uccello by Boeck (1931), followed by Marangoni. Salmi considers it by one of Uccello's pupils. A more likely attribution is the one suggested by Gamba (1909) and also considered by Pudelko, Longhi and Berenson. Pope-Hennessy attributes it to the Master of the Karlsruhe "Adoration"—a completely different artistic personality from Uccello. This artist certainly also executed the *Adoration of the Child* in the Staatliche Kunsthalle, Karlsruhe (see page 67), *Christ Carrying the Cross* in the Congregazione di Carità San Filippo Neri, in Parma, and probably other minor works.

Plate 124

SCENES FROM MONASTIC LEGENDS. Detail: plate 123.

Plate 125

SCENES FROM MONASTIC LEGENDS. Detail: plate 123.

Plate 126

PORTRAIT OF A LADY. *Panel, 58 × 38. New York, Lehman Collection (once in the Toscanelli Collection,*

Florence and then in the Aynard Collection, Paris). The portrait is supposed to represent Battista Sforza, wife of Federico, Duke of Urbino. It has been attributed to Uccello by Lionello Venturi, Lehman, Mayer and Boeck. Offner, together with Pope-Hennessy and Lipman, attributed it to the Master of the Castello "Nativity." Sirèn, Brockwell and Salmi (with reservations) ascribe it to Domenico Veneziano. The attribution to Uccello seems unlikely.

Plate 127

PORTRAIT OF A LADY. *Panel, 45 × 32. Boston, Isabella Stewart Gardner Museum.* It has been ascribed to Uccello by Van Marle (with reservations) and Lionello Venturi. Other attributions include: the Master of the Castello "Nativity" (Offner, Pope-Hennessy, Lipman), the Master of the Karlsruhe "Adoration" (Pudelko), and Domenico Veneziano (Berenson, Salmi). The last attribution seems the most probable.

Plate 128

PORTRAIT OF A LADY. *Panel, 63 × 40. London, National Gallery.* The work originally came from the antiquarian Egidi of Florence, who acquired it from the Casa Pancrazi in Ascoli Piceno. It has been subject to numerous attributions. Uccello (Morelli, Richter, Loeser, Van Marle, Boeck), Domenico Veneziano (Schmarsow, Lionello Venturi, Salmi), Antonio Pollaiuolo (Adolfo Venturi). An attribution to Alessio Baldovinetti, suggested by Fry, has been accepted by Berenson, Kennedy, Pudelko, Pope-Hennessy and others. In the 1951 Catalogue of the National Gallery (Davies) the attribution to Baldovinetti is confirmed.

THE ADORATION OF THE CHILD. *Panel, 110 × 47. Karlsruhe, Staatliche Kunsthalle.* In early times it was thought to have been executed by Pisanello. It was ascribed to Uccello by Loeser (1898), and recently Longhi seemed inclined to accept this attribution. Most critics believe it to be a work by a follower of Uccello, called by some the Master of the Quarata Predella. Others, following a proposal by Pudelko, think it the work of the Master of Karlsruhe. This artist is undoubtedly the closest follower of Uccello.

THE BIRTH OF THE VIRGIN, THE PRESENTATION OF THE VIRGIN IN THE TEMPLE, and THE VISITATION. *Mosaic. Venice, Basilica of San Marco, Capella Mascoli.* The attribution is based on documented evidence that, during his first stay in Venice, Uccello was engaged as a mosaic artist in St Mark's. Longhi (1926) has suggested that Uccello participated in the upper parts of the architecture in *The Visitation* (which Salmi thinks were renewed by Jacopo Bellini). Pudelko's theory is that Uccello executed the original cartoons for *The Birth of the Virgin* and *The Presentation of the Virgin in the Temple*, which were afterwards modified by Bellini who signed the completed work. Even though one can sense in Uccello's Venetian activity the presence of Tuscan elements together with a decidedly Northern character in the architecture, it is extremely difficult to determine to what extent Uccello participated in the work.

VIRGIN AND CHILD WITH TWO ANGELS. *Panel. Location unknown.* Published as a work by Uccello by Van Marle ("Eine Madonna von Paolo Uccello," in *Pantheon*, 1932, IX, pp. 375 ff.). This attribution was rightly rejected by Pope-Hennessy, who states it a work of the Florentine School but reserves doubts as to its authenticity.

VIRGIN AND CHILD. *Panel. Berlin, Staatliches Museen.* This panel is seriously damaged and has been repainted. Ragghianti suggested an attribution to Uccello. Pope-Hennessy ascribes it to the Master of the Karlsruhe "Adoration." Only careful examination of the original may lead to a definite assessment.

VIRGIN AND CHILD WITH ST FRANCIS AND TWO ANGELS. *Panel. Florence, Contini-Bonacossi Collection (formerly on the London market).* Published by Ragghianti as a work by Uccello. Salmi ascribes it to the Master of the Quarata Predella, and Pope-Hennessy links it to the Master of the Karlsruhe "Adoration." The last theory seems the most likely.

VIRGIN AND CHILD. *Panel. Washington, National Gallery of Art (Kress Collection). Formerly in Milan, Chiesa Collection.* The panel has been linked by Venturi, Suida and Perkins with the Prato frescoes (see comment on plate 24), but Pope-Hennessy's attribution to the Master of the Karlsruhe "Adoration" seems more likely.

A FEMALE SAINT. *Fragment of a fresco. Asolo, Church of San Gottardo.* Attributed to Uccello by Fiocco. This has been rightly rejected by Longhi, Salmi, Procacci and by Pope-Hennessy, who believes it a work of the Venetian School.

CAESAR'S VICTORY OVER THE GAULS. *Panel. Formerly Vienna, Lanckoronski Collection.* Schubring considers it the front panel of a *cassone*, executed by Uccello. The attribution has been rejected by Salmi and Pope-Hennessy, who suggest the style derives from Pesellino.

LOCATION OF PAINTINGS

AVANE (FLORENCE)

ORATORY OF THE CHURCH OF THE ANNUNZIATA

The Dead Christ Between the Virgin and St John the Evangelist (plate 60).

BAGNO A RIPOLI FLORENCE)

CHURCH OF SAN BARTOLOMMEO A QUARATA

The Adoration of the Magi, St John on Patmos, Two Kneeling Saints (plates 40–43).

BOSTON

ISABELLA STEWART GARDNER MUSEUM

Portrait of a Lady (plate 127; attribution).

CHAMBÉRY

MUSÉE BENOIT-MOLIN

Portrait of a Young Man (plate 121; attribution).

DUBLIN

NATIONAL GALLERY OF IRELAND

Virgin and Child (plate 39).

FLORENCE

DUOMO

Sir John Hawkwood (plates 10–11).
Four Heads of Prophets (plates 34–37).
The Nativity and *The Resurrection*, stained-glass windows (plate 38).

CONTINI - BONACOSSI COLLECTION

St Monica with Two Children (plate 33).

CONVENT OF SAN MINIATO AL MONTE

Stories of the Holy Fathers (plates 12–20).

CONVENT OF SANTA MARIA NOVELLA

The Creation of the Animals and *The Creation of Adam; The Creation of Eve* and *The Fall* (plates 1–9).
The Flood and the Recession of the Flood (plates 44–52).
The Sacrifice of Noah and the *Drunkenness of Noah* (plates 53–59).

UFFIZI

The Battle of San Romano (plates 80–91).
Sir John Hawkwood, drawing (plate 116).
Head of a Man in Profile, drawing (plate 117).
A Mounted Knight, drawing (plate 118).
Perspective Study of a Chalice, drawing (plate 119).
Perspective Studies of Two Mazzocchi, drawing (plate 120).

GALLERIA DELL'ACCADEMIA

Scenes from Monastic Legends (plates 123–125; attribution).

EX-HOSPITAL OF SAN MARTINO ALLA SCALA

The Nativity and the Annunciation to the Shepherds (plate 61).

LONDON

NATIONAL GALLERY
St George and the Dragon (plates 66–67).
The Battle of San Romano (plates 68–79).
Portrait of a Lady (plate 128; attribution).

LUGANO (CASTAGNOLA)

THYSSEN COLLECTION
Christ on the Cross with the Virgin and SS John the Baptist, John the Evangelist and Francis (plates 114–115).

NEW YORK

LEHMAN COLLECTION
Portrait of a Lady (plate 126; attribution).

ROCKEFELLER COLLECTION
Portrait of Michele Olivieri (plate 122; attribution).

METROPOLITAN MUSEUM OF ART
Portrait of a Lady (plate 23).

OXFORD

ASHMOLEAN MUSEUM
Hunt by Night (plates 100–105).

PARIS

LOUVRE
The Founders of Florentine Art (plates 62–65).
The Battle of San Romano (plates 92–99).

MUSÉE JACQUEMART-ANDRÉ
St George and the Dragon (plates 21–22).

PRATO

CATHEDRAL
The Birth of the Virgin (plates 24, 28).
The Presentation of the Virgin in the Temple (plate 25).
The Dispute of St Stephen (plates 26–27).
Blessed Jacopone da Todi (plate 29).
St Dominic and *St Jerome* (plate 30).
St Paul and *St Francis* (plate 31).
Clypei with Heads (plate 32).

URBINO

GALLERIA NAZIONALE DELLE MARCHE
The Profanation of the Host (plates 106–113).

WASHINGTON, D.C.

NATIONAL GALLERY OF ART
Portrait of Matteo Olivieri (plate 122; attribution).

SELECTED CRITICISM

(Uccello was) good and varied at composition; a great master in
the rendering of animals and landscapes; skillful in foreshortening;
and all of this because he understood perspective well.

C. LANDINO,
Commento alla Divina Commedia, 1481.

Paolo Uccello might have been the most original and inventive
genius in the art of painting, since Giotto's day, if he had but
spent half the time on drawing men and animals that he wasted
in the study of the details of perspective. For although these
studies are ingenious and beautiful, if a man pursues them too far
he wastes his time, exhausts his powers, creates difficulties for
himself, and often transforms fertility and natural skill into
sterility and constraint. And by concentrating more on these
details than on figures, his manner becomes dry and angular. All
of this is a result of examining things too minutely. Moreover,
he very often becomes solitary, eccentric, melancholy and poor
—as was the case with Paolo Uccello. This man, who by nature
had a penetrating, subtle mind, knew no greater pleasure in life
than solving almost impossible problems of perspective. Yet
although these were ingenious and beautiful, they hindered his
painting of figures so much, that the older he grew the worse he
did them.

G. VASARI,
Le Vite, 1568.

Ben fu nel pinger l'huom Paol felice;
Ma nel far gli animai col suo pennello
Volò tant'alto, che non pur d'Uccello
Cognome meritò, ma di Fenice.

"Paolo was quite good at painting men: but in painting animals

with his brush he flew so high that, rather than his nickname of
Uccello, he deserved the name of Phoenix."   R. BORGHINI,
                                                Il Riposo, 1584.

During the same period, as noted by Manetti, Paolo Uccello
was working [at perspective]. More than that, he dedicated himself to it, remaining only mediocre in other aspects of painting,
but excellent at this. He wandered in his studies, and often
repeated to himself how sweet a thing was perspective. This was
so true that, for him, novelty became a major source of pleasure.
Every single work that he executed threw new light on perspective; whether painting buildings or colonnades which were made
to appear large within a confined space; or whether painting
foreshortened figures with a skill that had never been attained by
Giotto and his followers. . . . [In the Chiostro Verde frescoes]
there is, moreover, a landscape with trees and animals, which is
so excellently painted, that the artist would have been entitled to
call himself the Bassano of the early ages.   L. LANZI,
                                          Storia pittorica dell'Italia, 1789.

Uccello had a sense of tactile values and a feeling for color, but
in so far as he used these gifts at all, it was to illustrate scientific
problems. His real passion was perspective, and painting was to
him a mere occasion for solving some problem in this science,
and displaying his mastery over its difficulties. Accordingly he
composed pictures in which he contrived to get as many lines as
possible leading the eye inward. Prostrate horses, dead or dying
cavaliers, broken lances, ploughed fields, Noah's arks, are used
by him, with scarcely an attempt at disguise, to serve his scheme
of mathematically converging lines. In his zeal he forgot local
color—he loved to paint his horses green or pink—forgot
action, forgot composition, and, it need scarcely be added,
significance. . . .
   A weaker man [than Masaccio] like Paolo Uccello almost
entirely sacrificed what sense of artistic significance he may have
started with, in his eagerness to display his skill and knowledge. . . .

Artistically, then, the naturalists, Uccello and his numerous successors, accomplished nothing. B. BERENSON,
The Italian Painters of the Renaissance, 1959.

If Uccello's temperament had been "calm and meditative," he probably would have come to executing perspective compositions. But he was, in fact, restless, playful and fanciful. Yet he attained glimmerings of perspective that dazzle one by their magical qualities. Certainly his results are serene, but they have the serenity associated with childhood: everything is transformed into a game, and everything is fanciful rather than contemplative.

Rather than errors in scientific perspective, the contradictions in the artist's perspective are the result of a *fragmentary* method of considering perspective. He presents different visions of perspective simultaneously, and these are related in only one way: by contrast. And this is also the answer to an exceptionally rich inventiveness, as it is to childlike fancies. Masaccio adopted perspective to suit his plastic concepts. Piero della Francesca sometimes managed to fulfill his soul in perspective. Paolo Uccello's position is different. The finer points of perspective are motifs with which he plays, but what really interests him is the playing. Playing is his form, and perspectives are his content. And Uccello can do what he likes with perspective for precisely the same reason that every artist is free to change his content.

This apparently highly experienced artist in perspective, this apparent founder of the science of art, was not a hero. He found his best equilibrium in limited works; he found his most spontaneous inspiration in superficial motifs, when he considered space as much as his soul. Then the poor fool was given divine inspiration. L. VENTURI,
Paolo Uccello, 1930.

Just as Piero [della Francesca] as an *artist* forms a perfect contrast to the pure intellectuality of men such as L. B. Alberti, so he is in contrast—a contrast which clarifies all the most intimate problems of a truly artistic story of style—with the *semi-artist* already visible in the dualism of his development that can be seen in Paolo Uccello. The latter was an artist whose character and inclinations were originally scientific and who, according to Berenson's wise essay, chose painting as his "organ." Despite a sure sense for tactile values—that is to say, artistic values— which were enhanced by a solidly founded schooling, Uccello never really managed to dominate his internal contradictions. Nor did he manage to attain a personal synthesis of Northern and Tuscan art, to which the events in his life would have led him. This is precisely because he never fully had an artist's nature, hybrid though it may be.

J. VON SCHLOSSER,
Prima Rinascenza Italiana, 1933.

With Uccello, on the contrary, it is not the subconscious but reason, starting from scientific knowledge, that is embodied in an abstract and fanciful world. And from what is accidental and changeable in reality it deduces what is eternal and perfect. We see him, in fact, as what he really is: a creator of an archaic, typified human race, as was Masaccio's, although different in its ethos; a creator of a stereometric race that lacks any individuality and is, in consequence, outside naturalism. Uccello appears to be, I repeat, essentially a Florentine and Renaissance artist. Nor can we weaken his will to create a form that is really *his own,* out of a Neoplatonic atmosphere in which man is "as God on earth," as Ficino said, because he is the author of his own world. In the difficult search of his spirit of artist-hero for an aesthetic ideal, Uccello was secretly proud to have penetrated into the essence of things. He was proud of giving them a simpler, more elementary life, a new truth of nature which, because it is immutable, finally becomes a supporter of classicism. Because of this, the artist belongs both in form and essence to the Renaissance, of which he remains its most unusual instance.

M. SALMI,
Paolo Uccello, Andrea del Castagno, Domenico Veneziano, 1938.

. . . the recent, fulsome apologies for his genius [Uccello's] are in the main swallowed by Surrealists who, sensing something irregular, mistake it for something esoteric. Even if the esoteric were present in this art (and it is only this that concerns us), it has to be read in every page and in every plate—not "between the lines" and even less behind every plate. A more certain assessment of this ingenious craftsman, this paradoxical "manufacturer of safes," will lead to another aspect of Quattrocento Florentine painting, an aspect that is less deceptive and more genuine.

R. LONGHI,
"Fatti di Masolino e di Masaccio," *La Critica d'Arte*, v, 1940, pp. 179–80.

Finally, then, Uccello's art is compounded of science and dreams, ability and ingenuity, contemplation and imagination. The inner life of the artist may admittedly be contradictory, but the contradictions should not be considered *per se*, as distinct from one another as the horses in the *Battles [of San Romano]*. Nor, for the sake of compromise, should their very nature be altered. They should be considered just as they are, but at the level at which they meet and agree, because it is at this level only that art is born. An art which creates rhythm by means of bisected space, geometrical forms, abstract lines, absolute colors, unreal light, of movement resolved in stages—such an art can have any and every psychological interpretation—dramatic, indifferent, ironic, ecstatic—because it has no predetermined psychology. Uccello had no need to determine the feelings of the subject he represented, because characters in stories do not have determinable feelings. If they have, this is not what interests them in any case. Besides, he did not realize he was creating stories. He was not playing about with motifs and the state of the human soul. He relived everything in the greatest serenity and conviction.

M. PITTALUGA,
Paolo Uccello, 1946.

It is very difficult to understand or assess this artist. One has the impression that all his works were executed accidentally, as it were, or as an experiment in the attempt to solve some problem or theory. Not as ends in themselves. Moreover, even their true artistic value and beauty seem expressed almost involuntarily

75

and the very quality for which we appreciate him comes to the surface casually, and not from any necessity. Indeed, one can take these ideas even further: in Paolo Uccello, as in Leonardo da Vinci, the man and his interests is something far more fully and profoundly intellectual than that which may be expressed in each individual work. And, in both cases, the works give one the impression of being only preparatory studies or marginal notes for some other, greater work that was never executed.

E. S. VAVALÀ,
Studi sugli Uffizi, 1948.

Like some settler pressing the area of cultivation on into the bush, Uccello extended the boundaries of painting. Within the context of the fifteenth century he was an innovator intent upon the task of reducing to order the world of visible phenomena, and of containing it, in all its bewildering complexity, within the confines of his picture space. But with the passage of time many of the symbols he employed in the interests of realism have ceased to appear realistic. *The Flood* requires exposition before it can be understood; the horses in *The Rout of San Romano* seem inanimate and motionless; and, like the fourth dimension of a fairy-tale, the device used for depicting space in *The Nativity* serves to suspend and not induce belief. Hence there are two Uccellos. One, the more easily perceived today, is a decorator who transports us to the realm of the imagination and builds up an irrational, patterned world, where warriors in fantastic plumes struggle in orange groves, and huntsmen, beneath a crescent moon, take part in a nocturnal chase. The other, less readily approachable, is the naturalist of the Chiostro Verde frescoes. And it is this Uccello, aspiring, compassionate and grave, who ranks with the great masters of Italian art.

J. POPE-HENNESSY,
Paolo Uccello, 1950.

BIBLIOGRAPHICAL NOTE

There is a great deal of literature on Paolo Uccello and, apart from various monographs, most of this consists of specialized contributions to reviews and periodicals in many languages. Although I do not always agree with everything they say, I wish to acknowledge my debt to two outstanding monographs: Mario Salmi's *Paolo Uccello, Andrea del Castagno, Domenico Veneziano* (Milan, 1938), and John Pope-Hennessy's *Paolo Uccello* (London, 1950). These monographs are recommended to readers who wish to extend their studies of the artist. Both contain numerous bibliographical references to individual problems.

The following list excludes highly academic studies. I have mentioned only the most lively and generally interesting critical works.

G. VASARI. *Le Vite*, edited by C. L. Ragghianti, Milan, 1947.

CROWE and CAVALCASELLE. *A History of Painting in Italy*, London, 1911.

B. BERENSON. *The Italian Painters of the Renaissance*, London, 1950.

C. LOESER. "Paolo Uccello," in *Repertorium für Kunstwissenschaft*, XII, 1898, pp. 83–94.

G. J. KERN. "Der Mazzocchio des Paolo Uccello," in *Jahrbuch der preussischen Kunstsammlungen*, XXXVI, 1915, pp. 13–18.

M. MARANGONI. "Osservazioni sull' 'Acuto' di Paolo Uccello," in *L'Arte*, XXII, 1919, pp. 37 ff.

F. ANTAL. "Studien zur Gotik im Quattrocento," in *Jahrbuch der preussischen Kunstsammlungen*, XLVI, 1925, pp. 3 ff.

R. LONGHI. "Un ritratto di Paolo Uccello," in *Vita Artistica*, II, 1927, pp. 45 ff.

P. SOUPAULT. *Paolo Uccello*, Paris, 1929.

L. VENTURI. "Paolo Uccello," in *L'Arte*, XXXIII, 1930, I, pp. 52–87.

R. LONGHI. *Piero della Francesca*, Rome, undated, pp. 20 ff.

M. MARANGONI. "Gli affreschi di Paolo Uccello a San Miniato al Monte," in *Rivista d'Arte*, XII, 1930, pp. 403–17.

M. MARANGONI. "Una predella di Paolo Uccello," in *Dedalo*, XII, 1931–32, pp. 329–46.

J. VON SCHLOSSER. "Problemi artistici della prima Rinascenza italiana: 3, Il semiartista: Paolo Uccello," in *Xenia*, edizione italiana, Bari, 1938.

W. PAATZ. "Una 'Natività' di Paolo Uccello e alcune considerazioni sull'arte del Maestro," in *Rivista d'Arte*, XVI, 1934, pp. 111–48.

G. PUDELKO. "The Early Works of Paolo Uccello," in *The Art Bulletin*, XVI, 1934, pp. 231 ff.

G. PUDELKO. "Paolo Uccello, peintre lunaire," in *Minotaure*, 1935, pp. 33 ff.

V. BOECK. *Paolo Uccello*, Berlin, 1939.

R. LONGHI. "Fatti di Masolino e di Masaccio," in *La Critica d'Arte*, V, 1940, pp. 179–80.

H. WASKERNAGEL. "Paolo Uccello," in *Pantheon*, 1941.

M. PITTALUGA. *Paolo Uccello*, Rome, 1946.

E. SANDBERG VAVALÀ. *Stuli sugli Uffizi*, Florence, 1948.

M. SALMI. "Riflessioni su Paolo Uccello," in *Commentari*, I, 1950.

R. LONGHI. "Il 'Maestro di Pratovecchio'," in *Paragone*, no. 35, 1952, p. 32.

E. CARLI. *The Whole Activity as a Painter of Paolo Uccello*, Milan, 1954.

M. MURARO. "L'Esperienza veneziana di Paolo Uccello," in *Atti del XVIII Congresso internazionale di Storia dell'Arte*, Venice, 1955.

G. C. ARGAN. "Paolo Uccello," in J. Lassaigne and G. C. Argan: *De Van Eyck à Botticelli*, Geneva, 1955.

E. MICHELETTI. *Paolo Uccello*, Novara, 1956.

A. PARRONCHI. "Le fonti di Paolo Uccello," in *Paragone*, no. 89, May 1957, pp. 3–32, and no. 95, November 1957, pp. 3–33.

E. SINDONA. *Paolo Uccello*, Milan, 1957.

R. PALLUCCHINI. "L'arte a Venezia nel Quattrocento," in *La civiltà veneziana del Quattrocento*, Florence 1957.

P. D'ANCONA. *Paolo Uccello*, London, 1960.

MARTIN DAVIES. *The Earlier Italian Schools* (National Gallery Catalogue), London, 2nd edition, 1961.

G. FRANCASTEL. "Découverte de Paolo Uccello," in *XXe Siècle*, Paris, December 1961.

REPRODUCTIONS

ACKNOWLEDGEMENT FOR PLATES

Alinari, Florence: plates 1–4, 6–11, 24–32, 46, 56–57, 61, 82–83, 88, 92–93, 111–113, 124, 125. *Brogi, Florence:* plates 5, 44, 45, 47–55, 58–59, 84–85, 87, 89, 90. *Gabinetto Fotografico della Sovrintendenza alle Gallerie, Florence:* plates 12–20, 23, 33–38. *Bulloz, Paris:* plates 21–22. *Giraudon, Paris:* plates 62–65, 94–99. *Archivio Fotografico della Pinacoteca di Brera:* plates 66–67, 122, 126. *Anderson, Rome:* plates 106–10. *Scala, Florence:* color plate IV. The remaining plates were supplied by the Galleries and Collections to which the pictures belong.

Plate I. THE CREATION OF THE ANIMALS, OF ADAM, OF EVE
and THE FALL, Florence, Convent of Santa Maria Novella, Chiostro
Verde

Plate 2. THE CREATION OF THE ANIMALS, Florence, Convent of
Santa Maria Novella, Chiostro Verde

Plate 3. THE CREATION OF ADAM, Florence, Convent of Santa
Maria Novella, Chiostro Verde

Plate 4. *Detail of plate 2*

Plate 5. *Detail of plate 2*

Plate 6. *Detail of plate 3*

Plate 7. THE CREATION OF EVE, Florence, Convent of Santa Maria
Novella, Chiostro Verde

Plate 8. THE FALL, Florence, Convent of Santa Maria Novella, Chiostro Verde

Plate 9. *Detail of plate 8*

Plate 10. SIR JOHN HAWKWOOD, KNOWN AS GIOVANNI ACUTO,
Florence, Duomo

Plate 11. *Detail of plate 10*

Plate 12. STORIES OF THE HOLY FATHERS, Florence, San Miniato al Monte

Plate 13. STORIES OF THE HOLY FATHERS, Florence, San Miniato
al Monte

Plate 14. *Detail of plate 12*

Plate 15. STORIES OF THE HOLY FATHERS, Florence, San Miniato
al Monte

Plate 16. STORIES OF THE HOLY FATHERS, Florence, San Miniato
al Monte

Plate 17. STORIES OF THE HOLY FATHERS, Florence, San Miniato al Monte

Plate 18. *Detail of plate 16*

Plate 19. *Detail of plate 17*

Plate 20. STORIES OF THE HOLY FATHERS, Florence, San Miniato al Monte

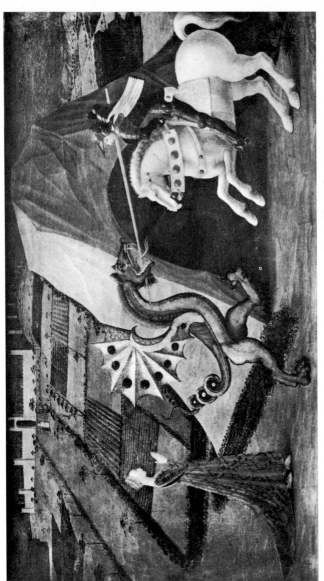

Plate 21. ST GEORGE AND THE DRAGON, Paris, Musée Jacquemart-
André

Plate 22. *Detail of plate 21*

Plate 23. PORTRAIT OF A LADY, New York, Metropolitan Museum of Art

Plate 24. THE BIRTH OF THE VIRGIN, Prato, Cathedral, Capella dell'Assunta

Plate 25. THE PRESENTATION OF THE VIRGIN IN THE TEMPLE,
Prato, Cathedral, Capella dell'Assunta

Plate 26. THE DISPUTE OF ST STEPHEN, Prato, Cathedral, Capella dell'Assunta

Plate 27. *Detail of plate 26*

Plate 28. *Detail of plate 24*

Plate 29. BLESSED JACOPONE DA TODI, Prato, Cathedral, Sacristy

Plate 30. ST DOMINIC and ST JEROME, Prato, Cathedral, Capella dell'Assunta

Plate 31. ST PAUL and ST FRANCIS, Prato, Cathedral, Capella dell'Assunta

Plate 32. CLYPEI WITH HEADS, Prato, Cathedral, Capella dell'Assunta

Plate 33. ST MONICA WITH TWO CHILDREN, Florence, Contini-
Bonacossi Collection

Plate 34. HEAD OF PROPHET, Florence, Duomo

Plate 35. HEAD OF PROPHET, Florence, Duomo

Plate 36. HEAD OF PROPHET, Florence, Duomo

Plate 37. HEAD OF PROPHET, Florence, Duomo

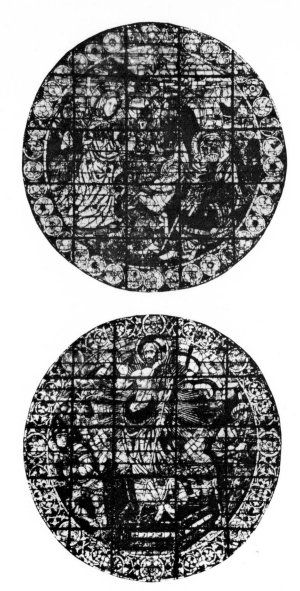

Plate 38. THE NATIVITY and THE RESURRECTION, Florence,
Duomo

Plate 39. VIRGIN AND CHILD, Dublin, National Gallery of Ireland

Plates 40–41. THE ADORATI*
(Florence), Church of

THE MAGI, Bagno a Ripoli
rtolommeo a Quarata

Plate 42. ST JOHN ON PATMOS, Bagno a Ripoli (Florence), Church of
San Bartolommeo a Quarata

Plate 43. TWO KNEELING SAINTS, Bagno a Ripoli (Florence),
Church of San Bartolommeo a Quarata

Plate 44. THE FLOOD AND THE RECESSION OF THE FLOOD, Florence, Convent of Santa Maria Novella, Chiostro Verde

Plate 45. *Detail of plate 44*

Plate 46. *Detail of plate 44*

THE FLOOD
Florence, Convent of Santa Maria Novella, Chiostro Verde
(*detail of plate 44*)

Plate 49. *Detail of plate 44*

Plate 50. *Detail of plate 44*

Plate 51. *Detail of plate 44*

Plate 52. *Detail of plate 44*

Plate 53. THE SACRIFICE OF NOAH AND THE DRUNKENNESS OF
NOAH, Florence, Convent of Santa Maria Novella, Chiostro Verde

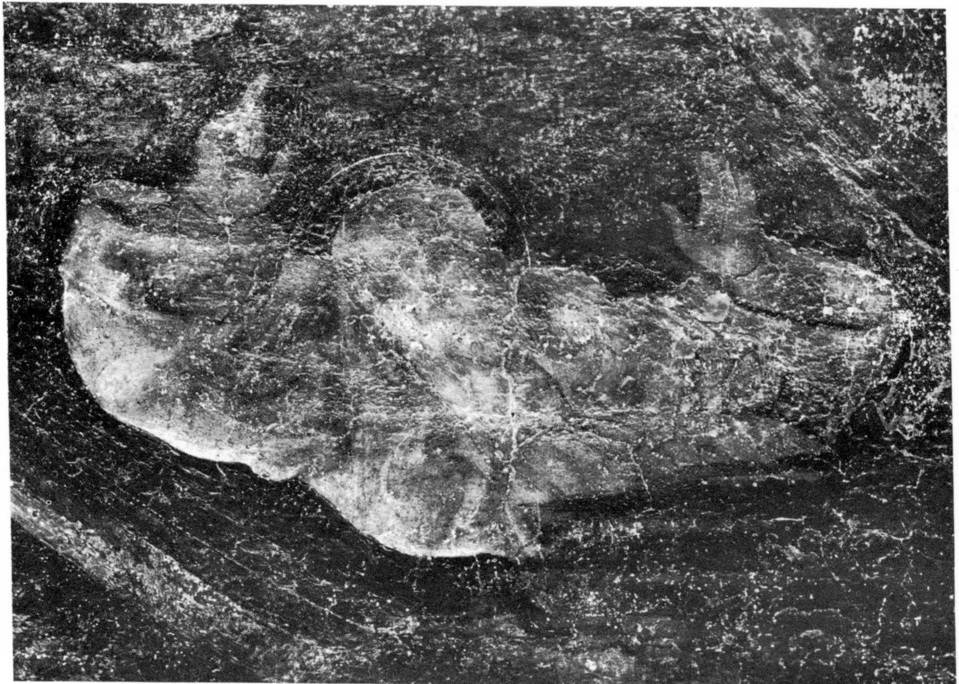

Plate 54. *Detail of plate 53*

Plate 55. *Detail of plate 53*

Plate 56. *Detail of plate 53*

Plate 57. *Detail of plate 53*

Plate 58. *Detail of plate 56*

Plate 59. *Detail of plate 56*

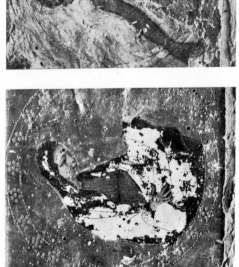
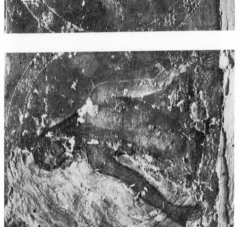

Plate 60. THE DEAD CHRIST BETWEEN THE VIRGIN AND ST JOHN THE EVANGELIST, Avane (Florence), Oratory of the Church of the Annunziata

Plate 61. THE NATIVITY AND THE ANNUNCIATION TO THE
SHEPHERDS, Florence, Cloister of the ex-Hospital of San Martino
alla Scala

Plate 62. THE FOUNDERS OF FLORENTINE ART, Paris, Louvre

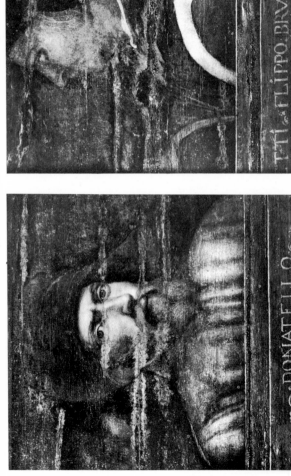

Plate 63. *Detail of plate 62*

Plate 64. *Detail of plate 62*

THE SACRIFICE OF NOAH AND THE DRUNKENNESS OF NOAH
Florence, Convent of Santa Maria Novella, Chiostro Verde
(*detail of plate 53*)

Plate 65. *Detail of plate 62*

Plate 66. ST GEORGE AND THE DRAGON, London, National Gallery

Plate 67. *Detail of plate 66*

Plates 68-69. THE BATTLE (

ROMANO, London, National

Plate 70. *Detail of plates 68–69*

Plate 71. *Detail of plates 68–69*

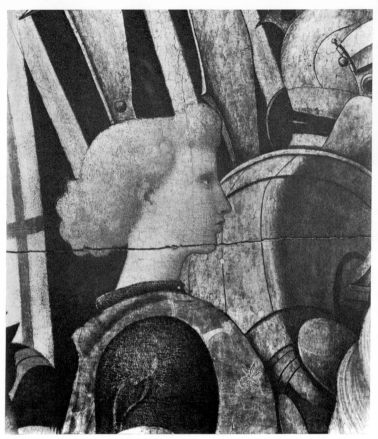

Plate 72. *Detail of plate 70*

Plate 73. *Detail of plate 70*

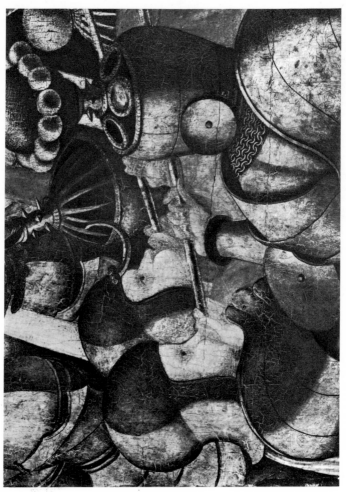

Plate 74. *Detail of plates 68–69*

Plate 75. *Detail of plate 71*

Plate 76. Detail of plates 68–69

Plate 77. Detail of plates 68–69

Plate 78. *Detail of plates 68–69*

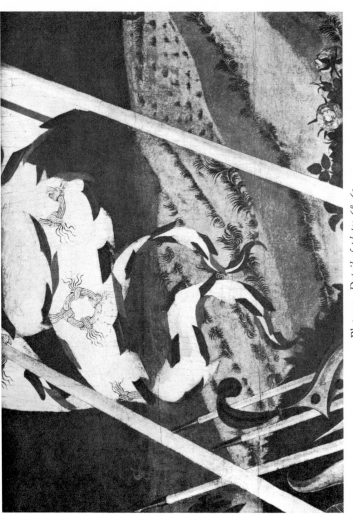

Plate 79. *Detail of plates 68–69*

Plates 80–81. THE BATTLE

N ROMANO, Florence, Uffizi

Plate 82. *Detail of plates 80–81*

Plate 83. *Detail of plates 80–81*

Plate 84. *Detail of plate 82*

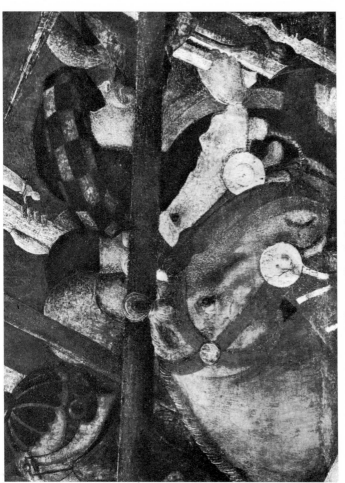

Plate 85. *Detail of plates 80–81*

Plate 86. *Detail of plates 80–81*

Plate 87. *Detail of plate 86*

Plate 88. *Detail of plate 83*

THE BATTLE OF SAN ROMANO
Florence, Uffizi
(*detail of plates 80–81*)

Plate 89. *Detail of plates 80–81*

Plate 90. *Detail of plates 80–81*

Plate 91. *Detail of plates 80–81*

Plates 92–93. THE BATTLE

N ROMANO, Paris, Louvre

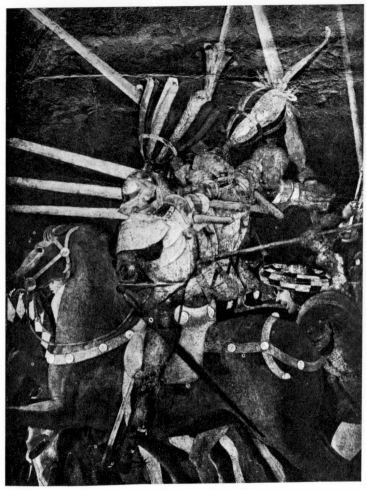

Plate 94. *Detail of plates 92–93*

Plate 95. *Detail of plates 92–93*

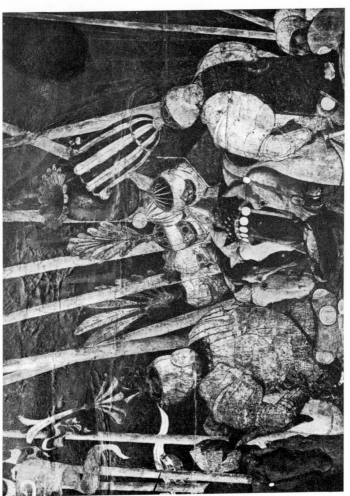

Plate 96. *Detail of plates 92–93*

THE PROFANATION OF THE HOST
Urbino, Galleria Nazionale delle Marche
(*detail of plate 106*)

Plate 97. *Detail of plates 92–93*

Plate 98. *Detail of plates 92–93*

Plate 99. *Detail of plate 98*

Plates 100–101. HUNT BY N

Oxford, Ashmolean Museum

Plate 102. *Detail of plates 100–101*

Plate 103. *Detail of plates 100–101*

Plate 104. *Detail of plate 103*

Plate 105. *Detail of plates 100–101*

Plate 106. THE PROFANATION OF THE HOST, Urbino, Galleria Nazionale delle Marche

Plate 107. THE PROFANATION OF THE HOST, Urbino, Galleria Nazionale delle Marche

Plate 108. THE PROFANATION OF THE HOST, Urbino, Galleria
Nazionale delle Marche

Plate 109. *Detail of plate 106*

Plate 110. *Detail of plate 106*

Plate 111. *Detail of plate 107*

Plate 112. *Detail of plate 107*

Plate 113. *Detail of plate 108*

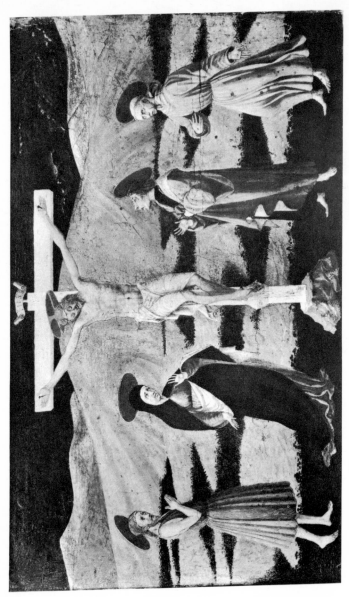

Plate 114. CHRIST ON THE CROSS WITH THE VIRGIN AND SS
JOHN THE BAPTIST, JOHN THE EVANGELIST AND FRANCIS,
Lugano (Castagnola), Thyssen Collection

Plate 115. *Detail of plate 114*

Plate 116. SIR JOHN HAWKWOOD, drawing, Florence, Uffizi

Plate 117. HEAD OF A MAN IN PROFILE, drawing, Florence, Uffizi

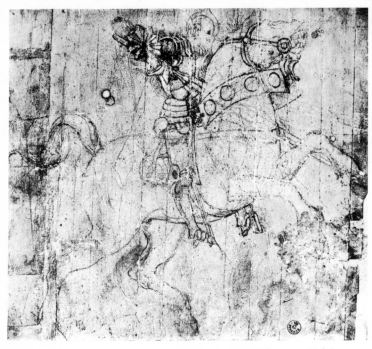

Plate 118. A MOUNTED KNIGHT, drawing, Florence, Uffizi

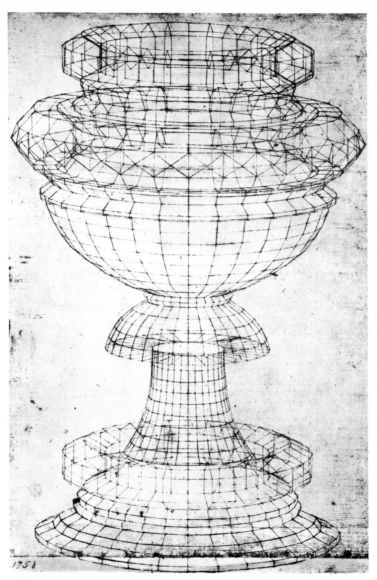

1758

Plate 119. PERSPECTIVE STUDY OF A CHALICE, drawing, Florence,
Uffizi

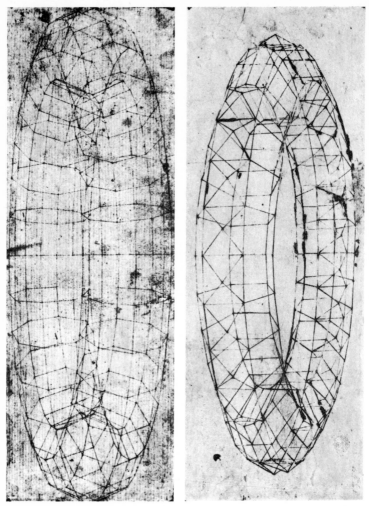

Plate 120. PERSPECTIVE STUDIES OF TWO "MAZZOCCHI,"
drawings, Florence, Uffizi

Plate 121. PORTRAIT OF A YOUNG MAN, Chambéry, Musée Benoit-
Molin (*attrib.*)

Plate 122. PORTRAITS OF MATTEO OLIVIERI and MICHELE OLIVIERI, Washington, D.C., National Gallery of Art and New York, Rockefeller Collection (*attribs.*)

Plate 123. SCENES FROM MONASTIC LEGENDS, Florence, Galleria
dell'Accademia (*attrib.*)

Plate 124. *Detail of plate 123*

Plate 125. *Detail of plate 123*

Plate 126. PORTRAIT OF A LADY, New York, Lehman Collection
(*attrib.*)

Plate 127. PORTRAIT OF A LADY, Boston, Isabella Stewart Gardner
Museum (*attrib.*)

Plate 128. PORTRAIT OF A LADY, London, National Gallery (*attrib.*)